Good Housekeeping
Consumer Guide

Home
Security
& Safety

Good Housekeeping
Consumer Guide

Home Security & Safety

Emma Burton

EBURY PRESS · LONDON

First published in 1995

1 3 5 7 9 10 8 6 4 2

First published in the United Kingdom in 1995 by
Ebury Press · Random House · 20 Vauxhall Bridge Road · London SW1V 2SA

Random House Australia (Pty) Limited
20 Alfred Street · Milsons Point · Sydney · New South Wales 2061 · Australia

Random House New Zealand Limited
18 Poland Road · Glenfield
Auckland 10 · New Zealand

Random House South Africa (Pty) Limited
PO Box 337 · Bergvlei · South Africa

Random House UK Limited Reg. No. 954009

A CIP catalogue record for this book is available from the British Library.

Editor: Alison Wormleighton
Design: Martin Lovelock

ISBN: 0 09 180688 7

Printed and bound in Great Britain by Mackays of Chatham PLC, Kent

Note: All prices quoted are approximate
and correct at the time of going to press

Contents

Chapter 1

Planning Home Security

In securing your home, there are two things you should aim to do. You should make your property as unattractive a target to thieves as possible, and you need to prevent – or at least delay – a forced entry into your home. Your greatest weapon against a burglar is time. The more barriers you place in front of him (such as fences and locked doors and windows), the less attractive your home will be. The chances are he'll give up and move on to the next house.

When considering home security measures, consider your lifestyle, what restrictions you are willing to impose on yourself and the practical aspects of any security devices.

Crime facts

- Every year, one home in 20 is burgled.
- On average, a house is burgled every 50 seconds.
- Over 50 per cent of burglaries take place in the evening or at night.
- On average, each of us will be burgled twice in our time as home-owners.
- Once burgled, you may have a repeat visit a few weeks later when the thief has calculated that you have received an insurance payment and have replaced goods such as your TV and video.
- Around 80 per cent of thefts are opportunist.
- Thieves are usually aged between 15 and 18 and live locally.
- On average, it takes two minutes for a burglar to go through your home.

Security check-list

Here are some of the further security measures you can take to prevent a burglary. All will be discussed in more detail in subsequent chapters.

- Fit a five- or seven-lever mortice lock and a high-security cylinder rim lock to your front door plus security bolts top and bottom.
- Fit a five- or seven-lever mortice lock to your back door plus security bolts top and bottom. Don't leave the key in the lock.
- Fit key-operated locks to downstairs windows and any accessible upstairs ones.
- Fit two locks to patio doors, top and bottom, plus an anti-lift device.
- Use timer switches on inside lights and on radios or TVs when you go out.
- Mark valuables with your postcode. Position valuables like TVs, clocks, silver, videos, stereos or computers so they are not visible through windows.
- Use good-quality locks or bolts on side and rear gates.
- Make sure ladders and tools are locked away after use.
- Keep hedges and fences low, particularly at the front of the house, so that a burglar can't work unseen. Use prickly plants to provide extra natural protection around your property.
- If going away on holiday, cancel milk and papers.
- Fit outdoor security lights. Key areas to spotlight are the front door, garage, shed, passages and any other obvious entry point.
- Lock the garage door. Consider replacing up-and-over doors with a high-security version and fit additional locks to the side posts.

THE AREA IN WHICH YOU LIVE

Burglary isn't restricted to poor urban areas, although the chances of being burgled are greater in some areas of the country than others. There are, of course, centres of high risk but burglary is a national problem. According to Home Office statistics, you are least likely to be burgled in Dyfed or Powys in Wales and most likely in the metropolitan area of London.

Be prepared when taking out house contents insurance for it to be affected by the level of crime in your area. You may not know whether you live in a high risk area but your insurers certainly will! The insurance premiums are usually based on your postcode.

Before investing in expensive locks, or other security measures, check with your insurers to see what they recommend. Some insurance companies insist on certain types of locks for normal domestic security.

BASIC SECURITY PRECAUTIONS

Often people admit they could do more to protect their homes and possessions but are put off by the cost. Yet many homes lack even basic security measures that cost little or nothing at all. Here are some initial steps:

- Don't leave doors and windows open.
- Use the locks already installed.
- Don't make it easy for the burglar: lock up tools and ladders.
- Don't 'advertise' what valuables you have.
- Don't advertise your absence.
- Ask neighbours to be vigilant (and you for their property in return).
- Ask your local crime prevention officer to visit your home.

POTENTIAL PROBLEM AREAS

Take a good look at your house from the outside, from a burglar's point of view, and consider how easy it would be to break in. Walk round the

---

Crime prevention officers

All main police stations have a crime prevention officer (CPO) who can offer advice on all aspects of crime prevention, including:

- the home (he will visit your home and recommend ways to improve household security)
- liaising with Neighbourhood Watch groups
- preventing car crime by suggesting anti-theft devices
- personal safety in the home and out and about
- bicycles (such as offering free cycle coding)
- presentation talks to local groups, for example, safe-driving courses aimed at women motorists

outside and make a note of all the potential weak spots. Ask yourself the following questions:

- Is the house secluded or hidden from the road?
- Do you live in a quiet, poorly lit or neglected area?
- Could a burglar work unseen behind high walls and fences?
- Is there easy access to the rear, such as a footpath or canal towpath?
- Do you have an open porch where a thief could hide?
- Does the house have side access which would allow a burglar to work unnoticed?
- Are the locks on your external doors adequate? Could you break the glass, reach in and turn the lock?
- Do you have valuables on display?
- Do you have a shed or garage containing tools, ladders, ropes, etc., that the thief could use to break in?
- If you have a garage (or coal bunker) with access to your house, are the locks adequate?
- Are your windows secure? Is there one that has been left slightly ajar? If there is, could you – or an agile youngster – reach it and climb into the house? Is there a window at the back of the house that you could force open, or break, without being seen? Is there a flat roof that you could climb on to, to reach a window? Is there a drainpipe or ladder left nearby that you could climb up?

All these features could encourage a burglar to target your home. But once you have pinpointed potential problem spots you can work out the best way they may be strengthened or corrected to make your house less vulnerable to theft.

How burglars break in	
Point of entry	**Method of entry**
Front door 33 %	Forced door or window 46 %
Rear/side door 26 %	Insecure door or window 22 %
Rear/side window 36 %	Break glass 25 %
Front window 9 %	Use a key 4 %
Upper window less than 1 %	Other 12 %

Chapter 2

Securing Your Home

One of the simplest and most effective ways to make your house secure is to fit good door and window locks. Once you have fitted the locks, you must get into the habit of using them. Establish a routine of checking the door and window locks before retiring for the night, and always lock doors and windows when you go out – even if you have just popped next door or down to the shops for a few minutes.

DOOR SECURITY

Doors are the obvious point of entry for a thief. According to the 1992 British Crime Survey, over 50 per cent of burglars got in through the front or back door. It's estimated that in 25 per cent of burglaries, life is made even easier for the burglar by the owner leaving a door open or unlocked.

Door locks

When you are buying a lock for a door, look for the BSI (British Standards Institution) Kitemark symbol on the front face of the lock and make sure the lock conforms to BS (British Standard) 3621. This ensures that the lock has been independently tested to prove its resistance to force, drill, hacksaw and picking.

Also look for a deadlock facility, which means the bolts lock into the extended position and can be opened only with a key. Because of this, a thief can't smash a nearby glass panel and then reach round and open the door from the inside, nor can he enter by a window and then leave by that door.

An anti-twist cylinder is also important as it prevents forced attack in which the cylinder mechanism is physically twisted out of the door with a screwdriver.

If in doubt about the suitability of your existing locks, check with your local crime prevention officer or a locksmith who is a member of the Master Locksmiths Association. They will also be able to recommend the types of locks you should have.

Most lock manufacturers now put helpful advice on the packaging of their products to indicate which door each would be suitable for (front/back, internal/external). There are two basic kinds of door locks:

Cylinder rim locks Also called surface-mounted locks or nightlatches, cylinder rim locks are fitted to the surface of the door and are used primarily as a convenient security lock for front or back doors. When buying a cylinder rim lock, it is important to choose the right lock for your particular need and application. Some offer a range of security and operational features. They cost between £30 and £70.

For glazed doors or for doors with a glass surround it is important that the lock has a lockable knob or handle. This prevents forced entry where the thief breaks the glass and reaches inside to release the lock.

For improved security, it is recommended that mortice locks are also fitted to supplement cylinder rim locks, particularly on front doors.

Mortice locks It is recommended that all entrance doors (front, side and back) be fitted with a mortice lock to supplement a cylinder rim lock. Mortice locks provide greater security as they are physically embedded or 'morticed' into the door itself. They are therefore less vulnerable to attack because they are more difficult to force out than a surface-mounted lock. They cost between £28 and £40.

Mortice locks are available with two-, three-, five- or seven-lever mechanisms. The higher the number of levers, the higher the number of key variations and the more difficult the lock is for a thief to pick. A typical British Standard five-lever lock can offer 1,000 key variations, whereas a seven-lever lock has over 6,000 variations.

Identifying mortice locks

To find out if you have only a two-lever lock (which is really too lightweight for the front and back door and only suitable for internal doors) look at the face plate in the edge of the door. This may be marked with the number of levers. If it isn't, look at the key. If it looks cheap or has very few notches then the lock is probably only two- or three-lever.

Front door

- The front door should be a minimum of 44mm/1¾ in thick. Check this, especially if you live in a flat with a communal main door. The door frame must be fixed firmly to the brickwork and be strong enough to hold the lock in place. The letter-box should be at least 40cm/16 in away from the locks.
- The front door needs a high-security automatic deadlocking cylinder rim lock with lockable internal knob or handle (to prevent entry by breaking glass and releasing the latch) and a five- or seven-lever mortice deadlock (to BS 3621). (A two-lever mortice lock isn't strong enough and should be used only on inside doors.)
- Fit a spyhole and door chain (about £6 each).
- Fit hinge bolts to reinforce the hinge side of the door (£4–£8 each).
- Fit door security bolts top and bottom. These are morticed into the door and locked into the frame for added security. The fitted bolts cannot be seen from the outside and are operated by a key from the inside. They can only be used when you are in the house, for example when you go to bed. One bolt, top and bottom, is recommended for external doors.

Back door The back of the house is the most vulnerable, with over 60 per cent of burglaries involving

Key precautions:

- Never leave a spare key in a convenient hiding place. Burglars instinctively know where to look.
- When you move into a new house, have the locks changed. You don't know how many sets of keys may be around.

Reinforcements

Don't forget, it's no use having a £50 lock if the door itself is of poor quality and can easily be forced. You can strengthen a door by using a door-reinforcement kit. There are many available, such as SecuStrip (around £30 from DIY stores, locksmiths and builders' merchants). It consists of two interlocking metal strips that are bolted to the door and frame (on the lock side) to protect against forced entry, even with the aid of a crowbar.

---

entry through a rear door or window, where burglars are less likely to be seen. It's therefore essential that your back door is as secure as possible.

- Fit a high-security five- or seven-lever lock (to BS 3621).
- Fit door security bolts top and bottom.

Patio doors Sliding patio doors are particularly vulnerable. Don't rely solely on factory-fitted locks for patio doors. Some can be lifted out of the frame, so for added security, patio door locks (£14) should be fitted to both the top and bottom of the sliding panel to increase protection against forced attack. You can also buy special anti-lift devices (£6) which fit in the gap between the door panel and the frame to prevent a thief from lifting the door off the runners. If the hinges are visible from the outside, the doors should have hinge bolts as well.

Glass-panelled doors These should be fitted with laminated glass, which is made of two or more layers of ordinary glass, bonded together with a strong, clear plastic interlayer. When attacked, the glass itself may break but the broken pieces will adhere to the interlayer and remain as a barrier. For further details contact the Laminated Glass Information Centre.

Who's at the door?
Most callers are genuine, but we've all heard tales of burglars getting into people's homes by pretending to be the gas man or from the council, so it's

sensible to be cautious. If you live alone, be especially careful.

- Identify callers by using your spyhole, if you have one fitted, before opening the door. Ask to see the identity card of meter readers, etc.
- For blind or partially sighted people, electricity, gas and water services can arrange for their staff to use an identifying password. If callers claim to be from local services, ask them to wait, shut the door and ring the office to check who they are. If you are unsure, call a neighbour or ask the visitor to come back when someone else is in.
- Don't keep a door chain on all the time. Only put it on when someone calls, otherwise it may be difficult for others to get in or out in an emergency.
- Don't leave your handbag or wallet unattended in any room that a caller may need to enter. Stay with a caller and keep all other doors closed.

Selling your house

Most houses are sold through an estate agent. If you are selling your house:

- Instruct your estate agent that viewing is by appointment only.
- If you're a woman on your own, ask your estate agent to be present when showing people around your house. If this is not possible ask a friend or neighbour.
- Although estate agents may demand that a 'for sale' sign be displayed outside your house, you can refuse to prevent unwanted attention.
- If your house is empty, make sure somebody keeps an eye on it. If you're unable to do this yourself, ask your estate agent or a friend.

WINDOW SECURITY

According to the 1992 British Crime Survey, 45 per cent of burglars got in through a window, with the back window being the most likely point of entry. An open window is an invitation for the opportunist thief. No less than 14 per cent of burglaries are made through a window that has simply been left open. Others are made by breaking the glass and reaching inside to release the window catch.

Window locks

Fitting effective window locks to your home will make your windows more secure against forced entry. Few burglars are willing to smash a window and climb through broken glass, and even a modest level of security is often enough to deter the opportunist burglar. No lock will prevent a determined burglar getting in, but it acts as a deterrent and will delay entry time. Yet fewer than five out of every ten households have fitted window locks.

All windows should have locks but pay particular attention to ground-floor windows and those above flat roofs, near drainpipes or near fire escapes. If you do choose to fit window locks on windows upstairs, remember to make sure that at least one window in each room can be opened quickly and easily and is wide enough to provide an emergency exit in case of fire.

Window locks are relatively inexpensive (about £3–£15) and are simple to fit. There are a number of different styles of window lock available depending on the type of windows you have and the materials they are made from. But all window locks are based on the principle of securing

---

By design

You can buy window locks for most types of windows.

Casement Outward-opening hinged windows should have a window lock fitted on the window frame opposite the hinges and secured into the central stile or side of the outer frame. For windows over 90 cm/3 ft high or 90 cm/3 ft wide, two locks should be fitted, one at the bottom and the other at the top of the window.

Sash To protect these windows it is recommended that sash bolts be fitted to secure the lower frame to the upper at either end of the mid intersection of the window when it is closed. Window locks can also be fitted on the side of both windows and secured to the main frame.

Sliding As with sash windows, sliding windows can be secured with a locking bolt where the sliding frames overlap when the window is closed or by window locks sited at convenient points where the window meets the outer frame.

the opening part of the window to the frame or sill by a simple bolt or clasp mechanism. Look for locks that have a detachable key. Remember to remove keys from locked windows, keeping them in a safe place out of sight and reach.

Window security tips

- When you go out, shut all windows – even small windows, like casement windows, skylights or bathroom fanlights. As a rough guide, if you can get your head through an opening, a thief can squeeze inside.
- Glue the slats of louvre windows in place with epoxy resin, or fit them with special louvre locks.
- Consider replacing the glass in vulnerable downstairs windows with laminated glass.
- Make sure there are no ladders left lying around that could help a thief break in through an otherwise inaccessible window.
- Install security grilles on vulnerable windows, especially at the rear of the house. Many DIY stores and ironmongers sell decorative grilles that can be attached to the wall quite easily with security screws.
- Roll shutters can be attached to the exterior wall, although they can be fitted on the interior if you do not want to change the appearance of your property. Both types are operated from the inside. They are usually aluminium or foam-filled aluminium, which also provides insulation. Contact the British Blind and Shutter Association for a list of local suppliers.
- Check that the window frames are in good repair. There's no point in having a good lock if the burglar can simply push in a rotten frame.
- Always have internal beading on double glazing, otherwise thieves can simply slit around the rubber seal and remove the whole window with a suction pad.
- For secure ventilation, especially if you live in a bungalow, use window limiters/child safety locks. These limit the window opening to no more than 15 degrees.
- When buying replacement windows look for ones that meet the new

BSI Kitemark scheme – Product Approval Specification (PAS 011) or Glass and Glazing Federation Specification for Improved Security 6.6. This ensures that they offer extra protection against forced entry by opportunist burglars. For further details contact the Glass and Glazing Federation.

OUTBUILDINGS, GARAGES AND GARDENS

There is a one-in-20 chance that something will be stolen from your garden in the next two years, whether it be power tools, plants or ornaments. Take a good look at the contents of your garden shed or garage. How much are they worth? £300? £600? £1,200? Probably more, so it's important to consider the protection of your outbuildings when taking precautions to secure your home.

Ladders and garden tools, particularly spades and forks, are often used to assist the burglar breaking into the house so make sure they are locked away after use and outbuildings are made secure.

If you have a garage with access to your house it is doubly important for the locks on the garage door to be secure. Consider replacing an up-and-over door with a high-security version or at least fit additional locks to the side posts. Position the locks as low as possible. The door from the garage into the house may be very secure but, once inside and under cover of the garage, a thief has got all the time he needs to attend to the door. He can't be seen and any noises will seem to come from inside. The thief could even use a drill to cut a hole in the door. Your neighbours could just assume you're doing a spot of DIY.

Padlocks

A strong padlock with an equally strong fixing point is essential. The effectiveness of the padlock is dependent not only upon the sophistication of its locking mechanism but also upon the quality of the fixing point or padbar. It is not much use having the most robust padlock if the fixing point is easily levered off or if the gatepost or door to which it is fixed is rotten or in need of repair. If possible, look for a padbar with concealed fixings or recessed bolts, as these give added protection against forced attack. There are two basic designs of padlock:

Open-shackle padlocks are the more familiar design where the looped shackle is exposed.

Closed-shackle padlocks have concealed shackles which make them less vulnerable to cutting or sawing attack. This type provides the best security.

Garden security tips

- Put away all tools and equipment and ensure that garages, outside sheds and store cupboards are securely locked when not in use.
- Store tools inside if you do not have a garden shed or outbuilding.
- Install automatic security lighting outdoors (*see* Security lighting, page 21).
- Use good-quality locks to secure your gates and doors.
- Keep hedges and fences low, particularly at the front of the house, so that a burglar can't work unseen.
- Check gates and fences for vulnerable spots, such as a low or sagging fence or a back gate with a weak lock.
- If you have a burglar alarm, consider extending it to cover out-buildings and sheds.
- Photograph valuable garden plants or ornaments for identification if stolen.
- Mark garden tools and equipment with your postcode using a hard-surface ultraviolet marker.
- Check that your household insurance policy covers theft from the garden and outbuildings as some policies may not cover this.
- Use prickly plants to provide extra natural protection around your property. Suitable thorny defenders include blue spruce, blue pine, creeping juniper, juniper, holly, Chinese jujube, firethorn.

SECURITY FOR FLATS

- As the front door of an individual flat is often not as strong as the main, outside door, it's worth upgrading a thin door with a more solid one.

- The door of a flat needs as many locks and bolts as the main communal door.
- If a fire escape runs up the side or back of the flats, make sure nearby doors and windows are secure.
- Talk to other residents, or the landlord, about installing a door telephone entry system. Bear in mind, however, that these aren't foolproof. Don't let anyone in for another flat or hold open the door for a stranger whose arrival coincides with yours.

NEW HOUSES

If you're buying a brand-new house, look for the builder's 'Secured by Design' symbol. This is a police initiative involving builders and architects to improve home security. It has the support of the Association of British Insurers, the Home Office and the Department of Environment.

The symbol is awarded to flats, houses and housing estates that meet police standards for home security to guard against burglary. This includes estate design, substantial door and window locks, security lighting, burglar alarms, secure boundaries and limited access to the rear. Only houses that are submitted are considered for the award. For further information, contact your local crime prevention officer or any builder displaying the 'Secured by Design' symbol.

Chapter 3

Adding Extra Security

The measures for improving window and door security discussed in Chapter 2, Securing Your Home, are your first line of defence against the burglar. There are, however, other measures you can take which will also improve security. These include installing security lighting and a burglar alarm, both of which should be carefully chosen to suit your own particular requirements. In addition, looking after your valuables by keeping them in a safe place, postcoding them and recording details of them will reduce the risk of loss. Your contents insurance will obviously be closely linked to the security measures you take.

SECURITY LIGHTING

Internal and external security lighting can play an important part in making your home safer and more secure. It can fool burglars into thinking the house is occupied and make it hard for intruders to approach unseen.

Illuminating dark corners around the house prevents intruders from using darkness as cover. The more visible the burglar is when he is trying to break into your house, the less comfortable he will feel. The element of surprise with automatic lighting may even be enough to frighten a burglar away. A burglar will also be less sure about whether the house is occupied if you have internal security lighting coming on and off whilst the house is actually empty.

Plug-in timer controllers

These can be used to switch lights, radios and TVs on and off whilst you are away to give the impression that the house is occupied. The most basic time switches simply plug into a socket outlet like an adaptor and into that you plug in whatever you want turned on and off – such as a lamp or TV. (You can't use time switches with fluorescent lights, but an adaptor is available for around £5.) They are simple to install and not too difficult to set. Several of them can be used around the home and moved around wherever you need them. They cost about £20. There are two basic types:

Electromechanical time switches are set by moving little markers or tappets around a dial. They operate, usually to the nearest 15 minutes, at the same time every day (or every week, with a seven-day timer) unless you move the tappets. Some switches will turn on and off at random within specified active periods.

Electronic programmable time switches can be set more accurately to the nearest minute. There may also be an option of setting different times each day.

Remember you will need to alter the settings as the days get longer or shorter. Also, unless an electronic time switch has a battery back-up, it will lose its setting if there is a power failure.

Security wall switches

You can fit a security light switch (about £20) in place of a normal light switch to control a central room light, wall lights or an exterior porch light. It will normally be set so that the light comes on only when it's dark, but methods vary, as do the levels of sophistication:

- Simple built-in photocells sense changes in light levels to turn lights on at dusk and off again at dawn.
- Passive infra-red (PIR) light detectors sense body heat, automatically switching lights on when someone approaches. Lights switch off again after a pre-set length of time.
- Switches can be programmed to come on and off randomly or at

predetermined times.
- Sound-activated switches automatically turn on a light when a sound is heard, turning it off again after a pre-set length of time.
- Some switches remember your on/off switching patterns over a 24-hour period and re-create the programme every day until changed.

Tip   Special light adaptors (about £20) that plug into a standard bayonet light fitting are a simple and inexpensive type of indoor security light. They automatically switch interior lights on at dusk and off at dawn even if the curtains are drawn.

Outdoor security lights

If you live in a large property, it may be worth considering illuminating large areas such as a drive or lawn with mains-wired floodlighting. This will spread an even, practical light, ideal both for deterring burglars from shady corners and for alfresco entertaining in the summer.

Alternatively, spotlighting smaller areas may be more effective and practical. Key areas to spotlight are over the front door, garage, shed, passages and any other obvious entry points.

Rather than having lights that stay on all night and require you to turn them on and off, consider installing passive infra-red (PIR) lighting. These only work when someone approaches your home. A passive infra-red sensor detects body heat within a certain range and automatically operates a light, turning it off again after a few minutes. The time the light stays on may be adjustable by simply turning a dial on the sensor, or it may be pre-set at the factory.

Most security lights have the PIR sensor incorporated into the light and there are various styles available, ranging from stylish globes and lanterns to more utilitarian bulkhead lights and halogen floodlights. Prices range from £15 to £50. Alternatively, PIR sensors can be bought separately and mounted away from the light – perhaps at the front of the house, turning on lights at the side and rear. They can also be used to operate existing lighting. Both types can be connected to operate more than one light.

Once the light is installed, you can usually adjust the positioning and

---

Safety warning

Unless you are competent at DIY, mains lighting should always be installed by a qualified electrician. There are strict safety standards for electrical installation to mains supply and you need a separate garden circuit with waterproof external plug sockets. For a list of electricians in your area, contact the National Inspection Council for Electrical Installation Contracting or the Electrical Contractors' Association.

---

the sensitivity of the sensor – important if it's close to a road or if you have pets. Some security lights can be manually overridden to allow the light to remain on or off if required. Most have a built-in light sensor to prevent daytime operation.

Lighting tips

- Don't forget that the wiring for outdoor lighting should be separate from your household system, with waterproof external plug sockets, and should incorporate a residual current device (RCD) and fuse. Installation should always be by a qualified electrician.
- Mount light fittings high so that no one can tamper with them. Adjust the sensor slightly off ground if you have cats or dogs, so they can't activate it accidentally.
- When positioning floodlighting or security lighting bear in mind that your neighbours may not want the night sky illuminated into the small hours, or a 500-watt bulb shining in their window all night. Be considerate.

SAFES

If you live in an area where burglary is common, a safe may be useful for small valuables and cash. Look for one that conforms to BS 7558. It's also worth checking with your insurers whether this will reduce your premium, and how much cover they will give for items in a safe.

Think carefully before buying second-hand (unless you are confident that the safe has been reconditioned to BS 7582). If you move into a house with an old safe, do not use it. Old safes may look quite secure but the technology used will almost certainly be outdated, making them easy to break into.

The most common types of safe used in the home are wall safes (about £50) which can be set in the brickwork or fixed to the wall, and floor safes (about £65) which are sited under the floorboards. You can buy small, free-standing safes (from around £120) but a thief may think you have something worth taking and decide to remove the whole safe.

It is important that the safe is securely bolted to the floor or wall and in a position where a thief would have difficulty prising it out. Have the safe professionally installed for maximum security. For a reputable company it's best to contact the Master Locksmiths Association.

To store and hide items such as money and jewellery, use a small portable unit, such as an SAS Security Can (about £10). These are cleverly disguised as household products such as shaving cream, furniture polish or tins of soup. They are available by mail order from SAS Products. Alternatively, Strong Point (about £35), a false double electrical wall socket, is available from DIY stores and locksmiths.

BURGLAR ALARMS

If after you've taken as many practical, physical and common-sense measures as you can, you still feel insecure, then it may be worth considering fitting a burglar alarm. This isn't a substitute for having good locks, but may be worthwhile if you live in an inner city or a secluded spot or have a lot of valuables. You will have to use it conscientiously, even if you're out for only a few minutes, as that is the major danger time for burglaries.

Don't be rushed into a decision by the offer of a discount, or by frightening stories of rising crime levels. You will need to discuss your security risks with your local crime prevention officer. Do not deal with doorstep salesmen of burglar alarms. You'll also need to think about whom you will appoint as your key-holders for occasions when you are away. You will have to give them – and your family – full instructions on using the system.

If you are considering installing a burglar alarm which is linked to a central monitoring station you must inform the police within 48 hours and give them the name or address of at least two key-holders. (Show the key-holders how to operate and silence the alarm.) The bell or siren should be set to cut out after 20 minutes.

For all other alarms, informing the police is not obligatory but is strongly advisable. There is no time limit.

It's also advisable to get advice from your insurance company before buying. Many insurance companies recommend that the installation of alarms be carried out by companies registered with the British Security Industry Association (the trade association), or the National Approval Council for Security Systems (NACOSS, the industry inspectorate).

Some insurance companies offer discounted premiums if you have an 'approved' burglar alarm system. But think carefully before trying to get a reduction on this basis, as it often involves you in regular maintenance checks by an approved company. Also, in the event of a burglary, if the alarm wasn't on you may have difficulty claiming. Don't expect any insurance discounts for DIY-installed alarms.

Costs of burglar alarm systems

A DIY-installed system from your local DIY or hardware store will cost from £100, depending on the complexity of the system (*see* DIY burglar alarms, page 31, for further details).

The cost of a professionally installed burglar alarm system will vary according to its level of sophistication. The installation charges will also reflect the nature of the house, such as its type and size, and the number of entry points. Expect to pay, on average, £400 to £700 for the installation and £35 upwards per year for the maintenance.

To ensure that you are charged the right price for the job, it is essential to obtain a minimum of three quotes from reputable installers before making your choice. Quotations are usually free and don't place you under any obligation.

Professional installers

The most expensive installation is not necessarily the best option. There are many factors to take into account.

- Check that the system meets BS 4737.
- Be suspicious of firms that offer you a ready-made package. For a burglar alarm to be really effective it needs to be tailored to your home and your particular needs. A professional installer should send someone to look at your home to determine what kind of lifestyle you lead so he can draw up the most appropriate form of protection before quoting. For instance, pets may cause a problem if allowed to run free in the area of movement detectors; if you are elderly you may have visits from grandchildren who are attracted to personal-attack buttons placed at low level.
- Don't forget to ask how much servicing and maintenance will cost and who pays if the system breaks down or there is a false alarm.
- You should also check that all equipment has a 12-month guarantee.
- Establish which part of the system you own. Signalling devices are invariably rented from the company. If the control equipment is rented you will lose this if you change alarm companies.

What system?

A burglar alarm consists of three main parts: the detection device, the control equipment and the signalling device(s). Think of an alarm system as a stand-in for you: the detection devices are your eyes and ears, the control unit is your brain and the signalling device is your voice.

Detection devices   These fall into two categories: fixed-point detectors and movement detectors. Which you choose depends on your circumstances and their application. For example, do not choose a vibration sensor (a type of fixed-point detector) if your house faces a busy road, or if your windows vibrate when it is windy.

Fixed-point detectors are normally fitted to doors and windows. There are three types:

- Switches that operate when a door or window is opened.
- Vibration sensors, which can be fitted on walls, windows or doors to detect physical vibration.
- Pressure sensors, which are hidden pressure pads that trigger the alarm when stepped on.

Movement detectors are normally fixed to the corner of a wall near the ceiling. These are four types:
- Acoustic, which sense airborne vibrations such as the sound of breaking glass.
- Passive infra-red (PIR), which react to a change in temperature as an intruder moves within a defined area.
- Air-activated, which sense changes in air pressure caused by doors or windows being opened or broken.
- Microwaves, which use high-frequency radio waves to detect movement.

Some alarms have dual-technology detectors incorporating two of the above detection methods in one unit. These help to minimise the risk of false alarms because both parts of the device must register an intruder. As the different detection methods respond to different parameters, the possibility of errors is reduced. Passive infra-red and microwaves are the most commonly used dual-technology detectors.

Pets cornered
- If you have pets, a burglar alarm system that works on fixed-point detectors as opposed to movement will enable you to confine the animals in one room but still use the alarm in the rest of the house.
- Some burglar alarms which use movement detectors have a 'pet-clearance lens' creating a clear zone at ground level to allow pets free movement without triggering the alarm. But, remember, cats have a habit of jumping on to window sills!

Hearing bells

- It's worth having a bell that sounds inside the house as well as outside. This is important as you may not be able to hear the outside bell, for example if you are in bed asleep. It also stops a burglar from hearing what is going on outside, making him more vulnerable.
- Remember that a highly visible alarm bell box will act as a deterrent, and if your house is vulnerable to attack from the rear, it may be worth fitting a dummy bell box at the back. You can buy spares at DIY stores.

The control panel This is the nerve centre of the alarm system and is usually situated in a cupboard or under the stairs. It must be accessible, but out of reach of young children and pets. Once activated by any of the detection devices, it sets off the bell/siren or alerts the central monitoring station (see below).

You should be able to set just part of the system, such as door, window and living-room detectors, at night when you are asleep.

Signalling devices

A bell-only system makes a noise when set off. It is designed to draw immediate attention to the break-in but relies on neighbours or passers-by to alert the police. Unfortunately, many people tend to ignore alarms and few actually report them to the police. Bell-only systems are sometimes fitted with flashing lights on the underside of the bell box. This gives a visual warning that the alarm has been activated, which is useful for identification within a row of houses with alarms.

Point to remember

Control panels and bell/sirens boxes contain batteries to keep the alarm working in the event of a power cut. These must be regularly replaced or re-charged (if possible). Alarm systems must also be regularly checked and serviced to make sure they are working properly. You should have a maintenance contract if you have a professional burglar alarm.

False alarms

False alarms make up over 96 per cent of all alarm calls responded to by the police in England and Wales, wasting millions of pounds in lost police man-hours per year. If police are called out to false alarms (with a monitored system) at your property four times in a 12-month period, you may receive a warning letter from the local police. If the false calls reach seven in a year, the police may stop responding completely.

• It's not just the police who are inconvenienced by false alarms: it could cost you, the householder, dearly too. If your system has been installed by an approved engineer, the British Standard requires him to reset the system once it has been set off, accidentally or not, in order to prevent burglars cancelling the alarm. Your insurance cover and premium may also be affected if police cover is withdrawn.

• Find out what caused the false alarm and put it right. There's nothing guaranteed to annoy the neighbours more than an alarm bell continuously and needlessly going off.

A monitored system is probably the most reliable form of alarm. When set off, it sends a coded message down the phone to a central monitoring station, which in turn calls the police or a nominated relative or friend (once it has verified the alarm is genuine). This system comprises a bell-only system with the addition of a digital communicator to link the alarm to the central monitoring station. All the major alarm companies run their own continuously manned monitoring stations. The police will accept calls signalled over the phone line from this type of system, provided the alarm company is approved (usually if it is a member of NACOSS). A list is available from crime prevention officers.

A personal-attack button is usually situated by the bed, with a second one by the front door, and you press a personal-attack button if you sense an intruder. It is deliberately operated by a push button and reset via a key. This device is used to activate the alarm at any time, whether the control unit is switched on or off. It is useful for the elderly or infirm, who can call assistance if in trouble.

On your wavelength

Certain radio frequencies have been allocated to DIY wire-free systems so that they don't interfere with the police, emergency services or cordless phones. However, interfering signals can sometimes prevent radio systems from working properly, and some systems don't show this is happening. Talk to other alarm-users and a couple of installers about the possibility of radio-frequency interference if you happen to live near public services.

The effective range of radio systems can be dramatically reduced by internal walls and floors especially if reinforced with steel.

DIY burglar alarms

If you are a competent Do-It-Yourselfer with experience in electrics, you will be able to fit your own system. Wire-free systems are the easiest to fit and should only take three or four hours, but you can also get DIY-wired alarms. These are cheaper but can take a day to install.

In a wire-free system there are no wires between the detection devices and the control panel. Each detection device contains a small transmitting device which signals to a receiver in the control unit. Apart from simplicity of installation, the advantages of having a wire-free system are that you can usually expand the system by adding detection devices, use the system to protect garages and a garden shed and take it with you if you move house. Their main disadvantage is that the police won't accept calls signalled from

Noise prevention

If there are no key-holders registered with the police, or available, local authorities' environmental health officers can obtain a warrant from a magistrates' court to enter your home to switch off alarms that have been sounding for over an hour and causing a noise nuisance. You may also be liable to a fine if you do not notify the police or key-holders.

Rather than annoy your neighbours through noise, co-operate in looking after each others' property by taking notice if the alarm sounds or if suspicious activity takes place.

them. Therefore they are restricted to local, audible signalling or signals to friends or neighbours by a coded message via the phone line. Look for BS 6707 on Intruder Alarms Systems for Consumer Installation. (Wire-free intruder alarm systems should conform to BS 6799.)

HIGH-RISK PROPERTY

The most attractive items for burglars to steal are portable, high-value goods – cameras, camcorders, TVs, videos, stereo equipment, computers – that can't be identified easily.

Property marking methods

If you mark your valuables, it will be harder for a burglar to sell your goods and easier for the police to return them, if they're found.

- For absorbent surfaces, such as documents or fabrics, use a non-absorbent ultraviolet pen, which costs about £1.50 from stationers.
- An easy way to mark hard surfaces, such as plastic or metal, is to use a hard-surface ultraviolet marker. Write in an inconspicuous place, as it's visible and can discolour some finishes. Eventually, the ultraviolet ink will fade and you will need to re-mark the items.
- For permanent marking, Domestic Pack (£8) from Selectamark Security Systems contains eight personalised stencils marked with your post code and house number. A special dye chemically etches these on to the item you wish to mark. The pack also contains warning stickers to deter thieves.
- Alternatively, you can etch your postcode, followed by the house number or the first two letters of the house name, on to hard-surfaced valuables using a special engraving kit available from DIY stores.
- Ask your local crime prevention officer for warning stickers indicating that your property has been postcoded, to display in the front and back windows of your house.
- Nationwide Property Register's Identitag kit is an effective way of marking valuables. The kit consists of ten ultraviolet identification and postcode tags which you stick on to high-risk items. Warning

---

Burglars' top ten

Don't assume you have nothing worth stealing.
This is what thieves like most:

1 Video recorders
2 Home computers
3 Cash
4 Stereo equipment
5 Chequebook, credit cards
   and documents (such as passports)

6 TVs
7 Jewellery
8 Gold and silverware
9 Cameras
10 Antiques

---

stickers are also supplied. Details of the items, including tag number
and location, make, model and serial number are stored on a database,
making your property easier to trace if stolen and later recovered by
police. It also helps in insurance claims, and, in fact, many insurance
companies provide details of it when you take out or renew house
contents insurance. The annual subscription is around £12.

Keep records

- Keep a list of your valuable items with the make, model number and
  serial number.
- Keep a note of your credit cards, cashpoint card, pension/allowance
  book, bank and building society account numbers and the companies'
  emergency telephone numbers so you can advise them of the loss
  immediately. Always store pin numbers separately from cheque and
  credit cards.
- It's a good idea to take colour photographs of jewellery, antiques,
  silver, etc., that can't be properly marked. Without an accurate
  description of stolen items there is little hope of their being recovered.
  It will also help in insurance purposes (*see* Recovering stolen goods,
  page 41).
- If possible, keep receipts for valuable items. It will help in the event of
  an insurance claim.
- Antiques can be registered with The Art and Antiques Recording
  Service. Photographic and written details of your valuables are stored

on a database. If they are stolen, the details are then circulated to the appropriate authorities. It costs £150 to record ten items, or the same price for 25 items if you supply your own good-quality photographs.

Don't make it easy for thieves
- Hide holdalls and suitcases in the loft, as thieves find them handy for taking valuables away.
- Valuables such as documents and jewellery should be stored in the bank when you go away on holiday for long periods, and items of lesser value hidden away. Most banks offer safe custody facilities, prices range from £10 to £50 per year depending on the bank and size of package. Check that your household insurance covers items whilst stored at the bank.

HOUSE CONTENTS INSURANCE

There are over 100 insurers offering household insurance, and all cover theft or attempted theft. There are two main types of cover:
Indemnity reduces the amount paid out when you claim, to allow for wear-and-tear and depreciation.
New-for-old cover pays out the cost of replacing an old item with a new one. Premiums are more expensive for this type of cover.

When seeking contents insurance, it is advisable to contact at least one independent intermediary to obtain a variety of quotes.

When you take out cover you will need to estimate the total, new replacement value of all your belongings. (The exceptions are linen and clothing. Nearly all policies make a deduction for wear-and-tear on these.) Policies often ask you to specify valuable items worth over £500.

Most insurers now insist on your having certain minimum levels of security before they will give you cover. If you improve the security of your home above their minimum requirements, some insurers will allow a discount on the cost of your home contents insurance. Contact your insurance company or broker for further details. Examples of improvements they look favourably upon include the following:

- Belonging to a Neighbourhood Watch Scheme.
- Having locks approved to BS 3621 fitted to all front and back doors.
- Having an alarm system fitted and serviced by a member of the National Approval Council for Security Systems (NACOSS). (Fitting your own DIY alarm kit won't reduce an insurance premium.)

Be sure to check your policy for exclusion clauses, however. If you fit security devices but don't use them, it may affect your cover.

Similarly, if you don't have a burglar alarm regularly serviced by a NACOSS-approved company or if it wasn't switched on at the time of the burglary, you may invalidate your policy and be unable to make a claim.

It's also wise to check your policy for holiday cover; leaving the house empty for over 30 days may restrict it. Check too whether the policy covers garden items as some policies may not.

FURTHER HELP

The Association of British Insurers issues a free leaflet, 'Beat The Burglar'. For a copy, send a stamped self-addressed envelope (*see* Useful Addresses).

Chapter 4

When You Go Away

It is easy for a thief to tell who's in and who isn't. The house may be in darkness, post left in the letter-box or milk bottles left out on the doorstep. One in ten burglaries occurs when a house is empty, so try to keep yours looking occupied when you are out or away on holiday.

THE LIVED-IN LOOK

- If you are going out for an evening, leave a light on in a room, not the hall (many people leave the hall light on when they are out), and perhaps leave a radio playing.
- If you are going away, don't leave your car full of luggage overnight. Load it just before you leave or lock everything in the boot or under the cover of the hatchback.
- Remember to cancel the milk and papers. Ring your local Royal Mail Customer Care Unit to find out if the Keepsafe scheme operates in your area. Under the scheme, Royal Mail will hold all your mail until you return home. (The scheme costs about £5 for two weeks, £7.50 for three and £10 for a month.)
- Curtains closed during the daytime make it look as if no one is at home. It is better to leave them open and get security lighting (*see* Security lighting, page 21). If you have a large number of valuables, it may be worth considering an electric curtain-track system. You can programme it to open and close your curtains at pre-set times.
- Mow the lawn before you go away.
- Buy a couple of automatic time switches for inside lights (from about

£20). These can be used to turn on a light, TV or radio at pre-set or random times (*see* Security lighting page 21).

- Don't leave valuable items like TVs, videos, stereos or computers visible through windows.
- Don't announce that you're going away to a shop full of people. Only tell people who need to know.
- Don't have your home address showing on your luggage for the outward journey. Put this only on the inside of your cases.
- Ask a neighbour to keep an eye on the house, collect post and free newspapers left in the letter-box, sweep up leaves, and even mow the lawn if you're going to be away longer than a fortnight. If they have two cars, perhaps one could be parked in your driveway. They might even be willing to open and close the curtains each day. You can repay the favour by doing the same for them when they go away. Warn the key-holding neighbour not to put your surname, address or even house number on your keys in case they fall into the wrong hands.
- If you're going away and leaving your house empty for any length of time, check with your insurance company what terms apply.
- A message recorded by a strange voice on your answering machine announcing that a guest is staying in the house while you are away will fool everyone except close friends. Never leave a message saying you have gone away or that nobody is at home to take the call.
- Just before setting off on holiday, it's worth spending a quiet couple of minutes on the doorstep to check you've done everything.

HOME SITTERS

The enjoyment of a holiday is often marred by worrying about the possibility of your home being burgled in your absence. Although you may be able to enlist the help of neighbours to a degree, it could be worth considering a professional home sitter if you have pets or a conservatory full of precious plants. Some insurance companies will allow a discount on your premiums if you use a home sitter; check with your insurers for details.

Obviously you don't want just anyone living in your home, so be sure to choose a professional company that:

- has been in business a reasonable length of time
- is registered and licensed by the Department of Employment
- vets its home sitters/caretakers carefully and takes references
- is comprehensively insured against any problems that might occur such as the home sitter having an accident, simply not being up to the task, or damaging your home
- provides full back-up for the home sitter so that if he/she falls ill, or has to leave the assignment, the company is still bound to honour the contract.

Of the larger companies, Homesitters employs all its people (charges include all PAYE and National Insurance contributions), while Universal Aunts and Animal Aunts are agencies that link self-employed sitters to homeowners. A sitter for two weeks will cost around £250 to £300 depending on your requirements (excluding travelling expenses and food).

Tip For peace of mind, meet the prospective home sitter/caretaker before the day you hand over the keys.

Watch it!

Setting up or joining a Neighbourhood Watch or Street Watch group can help reduce the level of crime and the fear of crime in a neighbourhood. In some areas crime is claimed to have been reduced by 75 per cent. The schemes do not encourage people to set up as a vigilante group, but just to be on the lookout for suspicious behaviour and to enhance the security of members' properties.

If there isn't a scheme operating in your area and you're interested in setting up your own group, find out first whether others share your enthusiasm and then approach your local police. Further information on Neighbourhood Watch and Street Watch is provided in a Home Office booklet, 'Partners Against Crime'. For a free copy, ring 01345-235235.

Chapter 5

If You Are Burgled

If you find you have been burgled, call the police immediately. Even if you can't give accurate details, the police will respond. While waiting for them to arrive, don't move or touch anything especially at the point of entry/exit or items that have been moved, except to minimise any damage. Fingerprints may provide vital clues in helping to trace the thief. Give details of any valuables that have been stolen to the police when they arrive.

If you arrive home and think you have been burgled (because of an open door or broken window) and you suspect that the burglar could still be in your house, don't go inside. Go to a neighbour's house or a phone box and ring the police, then keep a discreet watch so you can give the police a description of anyone leaving.

Coming face to face with a burglar
If you find an intruder in the house with you:
- ask calmly what he wants;
- don't get angry or attempt to prevent him from leaving: he may get violent;
- try to remember what he looks like in as much detail as possible;
- call the police as soon as he has gone.

If you suspect a prowler
If you hear a noise as though someone is in the house, or someone is trying to break in, do the following:

- Switch the lights on and make plenty of noise. Most burglars will flee immediately.
- Stay upstairs or out of the way, call the police if you have a bedroom phone extension and find something you can use as a weapon to defend yourself if you are attacked – but don't go in search of him. If you can't get to a phone, stay put until the thief has left and it's safe to move.
- As soon as you hear the intruder leave, try to see what he looks like and what he is wearing, which way he goes and whether he has a car or van. Then ring the police.

Tip If you get a good look at an intruder, try to memorise details to help the police: age, sex, height, build, skin colour, hairstyle and colour, facial characteristics, clothing. For vehicles, note the type, model, colour and registration number.

Community alarms

For the elderly or disabled who may not be able to reach a telephone during a break-in, a community alarm can be fitted. The alarm works as a normal telephone with the additional feature that it can automatically dial a control centre (run by local housing authorities, social services departments or commercial monitoring companies). It is triggered by pressing a button on the telephone or on a pendant worn around the neck. Prices for this service vary from free to less than £5 a week. Contact your local housing authority, social services or Help the Aged. (Help the Aged also produce an advice leaflet, 'Security In Your Home'.)

MAKING A HOME-INSURANCE CLAIM

If, unfortunately, you have to make a claim on your home insurance, here is how to make the process as smooth and fast as possible:

- Read your policy carefully. Does it cover the cause of the damage or loss? Should you claim under 'buildings' or 'contents'?
- Ring your insurers and ask for a claim form, quoting your policy

number. Quote your policy number on all correspondence, and keep copies.

- If temporary emergency repairs are needed, arrange these immediately and let your insurers know. The cost may form part of your overall claim, so keep all the bills and any damaged items, as the insurers will probably want to see them. Take photos if necessary. Some insurers offer a 24-hour emergency help-line which can give details of local tradespeople.

- Whilst waiting to receive a claim form, get repair estimates from at least two specialist contractors, list all items lost or damaged, and find the original receipts if you can. If you can't, estimate their current value and check the price of replacements. Some policies offer replacement as if the items had been new, whilst others take wear-and-tear into account (*see* House contents insurance, page 34).

- Complete the claim form and return it quickly, with any estimates, receipts and valuations.

- The insurers will pay your claim, arrange for their claims inspector to call on you, or send a loss adjuster to assess the loss or damage.

RECOVERING STOLEN GOODS

If your home has been burgled, the chances of your ever seeing your most valuable belongings again are, realistically, rare. If items are security-marked, the chances increase considerably, and if you have photographs and detailed descriptions of precious items, even better. If the items are antiques, it may be worth contacting one of the following:

- *The Antiques Trade Gazette*, a weekly newspaper with a section on stolen goods is circulated to the antiques trade internationally.

- *Trace* magazine publishes details of stolen works of art and antiques. Around 60 per cent of its advertisements are placed by private individuals.

- The Art Loss Register keeps a permanent database of stolen art and antiques which is checked against auction catalogues. Any item worth over £500 in value can be registered for £20.

Chapter 6

Car Security

With the current spate of joyriding, carjacking and mobile-phone theft, car crime now accounts for more than a quarter of all recorded crime in the UK. According to the 1994 British Crime Survey, over four million private cars were stolen, or stolen from, in 1993, yet 70 per cent of cars have no security devices fitted and one in eight drivers sometimes don't lock their cars. As well as causing frustration and inconvenience, theft can cost you dearly in repairs, car rental and increased insurance premiums.

IS YOUR CAR AT RISK?

The chances of having your car stolen or broken into depend on such factors as the model, where you live and where the car is parked.

Car crime facts

- A car is stolen every minute.
- It can take just four seconds for a thief to break into a car without a key.
- Almost a third of all car thefts, and thefts from cars, occur in car parks.
- About one in four of the cars reported missing each year is never recovered.
- It is estimated that nearly two-thirds of cars are stolen for one-off use, either for joyriding or for use in another crime.
- Thefts from cars are a major problem. In 1993 there were over 2.5m thefts from vehicles.
- One in five vehicle owners is a victim of some sort of car crime.
- According to a Home Office survey, 12 per cent of vehicle owners admitted to sometimes leaving their car unlocked.
- A third of all car thefts took place in the street near home at night.

High-risk vehicles

It's a well-known fact that some cars are more attractive to thieves than others. In fact, some insurers won't even provide cover for certain models of car unless you take particular security precautions. These include four-wheel-drive 'off-road' vehicles such as the Range Rover, Ford Escort XR3i, Volkswagen Golf GTI and Sierra Cosworth. The cars which are favourite targets for thieves tend to be the more expensive sporty models, especially high-performance versions of popular family cars.

Where you live

According to the 1992 British Crime Survey, if you live in one of the 'poorest council estates', you're ten times more likely to have your car stolen than if you live in the countryside. Inner-city areas are also high-risk.

Where you park

You can lessen the risks of theft by parking your car in a garage. Home Office research shows that parking your car in the garage is 20 times safer than parking it in a driveway and 50 times safer than parking it in a street.

Your car is most likely to be targeted by a thief when it is parked near your home. More than half of cars stolen or broken into were parked near home and nearly all these incidents were in the evening or during the night.

VEHICLE SECURITY DEVICES

Simple and often inexpensive methods of improving the security of your car can make an enormous difference in reducing the risks of theft. Whether you spend £20 on a steering wheel lock or £400 on a combined alarm/immobiliser depends on what value you place on your car, where you keep it, where you live and whether you think you will be able to use the device every time you leave the car. Few, except the most sophisticated of devices, will thwart the determined thief, but if you can prolong the time it takes him to break in or to drive off, he may think twice.

Alarms

Car alarms may be DIY or professionally installed. They offer different levels of protection, convenience and sophistication, depending on price. To deter a thief from attempting to steal the car or its contents, an alarm will sound a siren and flash car lights. In general, the more expensive the system, the more sensors or levels of protection it will provide and hence the greater the deterrent value. Prices range from £50 to £200. They should conform to BS 6803, so check before you buy.

Advantages
- They deter opportunist and inexperienced thieves.
- They alert you to a break-in, if you are within earshot.
- Some alarms come with a pager to alert you to tampering.

Disadvantages
- Car alarms are often ignored.
- An alarm alone won't stop a thief from driving away.
- DIY alarms can be very complicated to install and, unless fitted correctly, will probably be more prone to false alarm.

Electronic immobilisers

Immobilisers are intended to prevent theft of the vehicle and operate by preventing a part or several parts of the engine from working. They are generally very sophisticated and are therefore expensive, costing from £120 to £400. Although you can fit one yourself, the RAC and AA are against amateurs fitting an immobiliser because of concerns about safety.

Immobilisers are permanently built into the vehicle and will generally be much more convenient to use as well as requiring more time and effort on the part of the thief in order to overcome them.

Advantages
- They deter joyriders.
- A thief would take longer to overcome an immobiliser than an alarm.

Disadvantages
- They do not prevent the theft of car contents.

Combined alarm/immobilisers

Although expensive, priced from £250 to £700, a combined alarm/immobiliser offers the best protection, deterring the thief from attempting to steal both the car and its contents.

Mechanical locking devices

These generally act as a visual deterrent to the casual thief. They are best suited to older, low-risk or low-value cars or to use in conjunction with other security devices such as a good alarm system.

Approved vehicle security devices

There is currently no British Standard for combined alarm/immobilisers, electronic immobilisers or mechanical locking devices. In order to ensure that vehicle security devices are effective, the insurance industry has set up its own approval scheme, backed by the Association of British Insurers and Lloyd's of London. They have set standards which the combined alarm/immobilisers, electronic immobilisers and mechanical locking devices must meet to gain their approval. These are tested at the Motor Insurance Repair Research Centre, Thatcham.

Insurance companies may specify the use of the approved systems as a basis for discounts or as a requirement before insurance can be taken out or renewed. Check with your insurance company for further details. A full list of approved security devices is regularly updated; for a copy contact the Association of British Insurers.

A similar scheme, set up by Northumbria Police, has been so successful that it is now being adopted by all other forces around Britain. Under the scheme, called 'Sold Secure – Partnership Against Car Theft', vehicle security devices (mostly professionally fitted) must pass a five-minute attack test. Outlets selling a recognised product will issue a certificate to show that a device has passed this. To find out which devices meet SSPACT's criteria, contact the Sold Secure Office. Also look out for the SSPACT logo on product packaging.

They cost from £7 to £200 and there is a wide variety available, from steering wheel and gear-lever locks to wheel clamps. The most important consideration is how easy it is for you to fit and remove them. If you don't think that you could be bothered to fit and subsequently remove the device every time you leave the car and no matter how brief your absence from it, then the product isn't worth buying.

Advantages
- They are visible deterrents.
- They prolong the amount of time it would take for a thief to drive the car away.

Disadvantages
- They won't stop a very determined, expert thief.
- They need refitting every time you leave your car.
- They do not prevent the theft of car contents.
- Professional car thieves can remove most steeringwheel locks in a few seconds.

Accredited installers

Even approved security devices can't be effective if incorrectly installed, so when you're having alarms and immobilisers professionally fitted, find a reputable installer who offers a guarantee. Look out for the Vehicle Security Installation Board (VSIB) logo. This indicates that the fitter meets the VSIB's code of practice to ensure security devices are properly fitted. The scheme has the support of many organisations including the insurance industry, AA, RAC and car manufacturers.

As with approved devices, insurance companies may specify VSIB-approved installation before offering discounts. Check with your insurance company for further details. For a full list of accredited installers, contact the Association of British Insurers.

VEHICLE SECURITY INSTALLATION BOARD

BUYING NEW

If you are buying a brand new car, you will have a choice of security features. Some car manufacturers have responded to the need for greater security, and more and more new cars are fitted with anti-theft devices as standard items (or as an option). According to the Society of Motor Manufacturers and Traders, 77 per cent of new models now have central locking systems and 95 per cent offer alarms as standard or optional. In addition, 22 per cent of new cars are now fitted with dead-locking or double-locking as standard, which prevents doors from being opened without a key even when windows are smashed or left open. When you buy, look out for:

- an immobilising device
- a car alarm fitted as standard
- a visible VIN (vehicle identification number) – a deterrent against professional thieves intending to change the vehicle's identity
- car doors fitted with deadlocks
- a central locking system
- removable or security-coded car radio–cassette player
- lockable fuel cap and wheel nuts
- etched windows and security-marked panels/equipment

CAR-SPOTTING SYSTEMS

If your car has been stolen, the chances of recovering it are small. One in four stolen cars is never found. If your car is very high risk then you should consider supplementing a combined alarm/immobiliser with a tracking device. They are costly, however. There are currently two systems widely available. Both systems must be professionally installed.

The Tracker system incorporates a transmitter hidden in the car. If you report the stolen car to the Tracker network, the police can use a tracking device fitted in their cars to find yours. The system costs about £199 including fitting plus £61 for a year's subscription. Alternatively, drivers can buy the system outright for £399. It's AA-endorsed. Call the AA free on 0800 990099 for further details.

The TrakBak system is more sophisticated, as the transmitter installed in the vehicle is linked to an engine immobiliser. The TrakBak control centre monitors the whereabouts of the vehicle the moment it is stolen – even if the thief overrides the immobiliser and the vehicle is 'hoisted' away. It contacts you to verify that your vehicle has been stolen, and alerts the police to its location. Once recovered, your car will then be returned to you as part of the service. The system costs £850 including fitting plus £141 for a year's subscription. Contact Securicor TrakBak for further details.

Tip   Many insurance companies offer discounted premiums if you have these devices fitted. Check with your insurance company or broker for details.

CAR SECURITY PRECAUTIONS

- Engrave windows, wing mirrors, radios, etc., with the car registration number. Your local police or garage may arrange etching sessions. As well as making your property easier to trace if stolen, this acts as a deterrent. Use stickers to warn thieves. Etching should comply with BS AU209/3.
- Fit an anti-theft device and use it every time you park.
- Fit lockable wheel nuts, especially if you have alloy wheels. They cost around £14 and are available from car dealers. You have to know the car's make, model and year.
- If you're buying a radio–cassette player, buy one that can be removed by the owner or that has security coding. Security-mark it with an ultraviolet pen and make a note of the serial number.
- If possible, look for well-supervised car parks with restricted entry and exit points, good lighting and security cameras (*see* Car parks, page 60).
- Don't leave valuables (handbags, briefcases, cameras, mobile phones, etc.) on show. If you can't take them with you, lock them in the boot.
- Don't leave credit cards or chequebooks in the glove compartment – one in five stolen plastic cards is taken from a car.

- Fit a lockable fuel cap. This stops a thief from stealing petrol, and joyriders may be forced to abandon a vehicle when it runs out of fuel.
- Always lock your car and engage the steering lock even if you're only leaving it for a few minutes. For example, when filling the car with petrol. Never leave the keys in the ignition.
- Never leave a window or a sunroof open.
- Put your aerial down when you park to stop it being vandalised.
- Never leave vehicle documents in your car. They could help a thief sell your car.
- The safest place to park your car is your garage. If you don't have a garage, choose a busy, well-lit area. If you're parking in daylight but returning to your car at night, think how things will look in the dark.

CAR INSURANCE

It is an offence to drive your car or allow others to drive it without insurance. Various factors are taken into account in deciding how much your insurance will cost, including the drivers, the type of car, where it is kept and what it is used for, as well as the type of cover required. Decide which type of cover you need.

Third party only covers liability for injuries and damage to other persons or their property.

Third party fire and theft covers as above plus loss to your car by fire or theft.

Comprehensive covers third party fire and theft risks plus accidental damage to your own car. Additional benefits may be included, such as windscreen cover and cover for personal belongings. Premiums are more expensive – roughly double the third party fire and theft premium.

Tip Many insurance companies offer discounts on car insurance premiums if you fit an approved anti-theft device, such as an alarm or immobiliser (*see* Vehicle security devices, page 43). Further discounts may be offered for other security measures, such as keeping your car in a locked garage. Contact your insurance company or broker for further details.

Chapter 7

Bicycle Security

Like the vast majority of crimes in Britain today, cycle theft is on the increase. Over 170,000 bicycles are reported stolen every year, although the total number of bike thefts is estimated to be much higher. Bikes are a popular target because they can easily be sold. The trend for expensive mountain bikes has added to the temptation. By taking a few simple precautions you can ensure that your bike is as well protected as possible.

CYCLE LOCKS AND ALARMS

Buying a good cycle lock is the best way to protect your bike. No lock can protect your bike from the determined thief; at best it will help slow one down. But some locks are better at deterring and delaying a thief than others. In the main, the more you spend on a lock, the better the level of security. There are three main types of lock:

Coil and cable locks are usually plastic-coated steel wire or cable. They're inexpensive (from around £5), light and easy to use since they are fairly flexible, but are easily cut. They are best used for short-term parking in low-risk locations or for securing a cycle helmet to the bike.

Chain and padlock systems have chains which can be snipped through in seconds, although the heavier and more expensive systems (around £35) tend to be more secure.

Shackle locks are also called 'U' or 'D' locks and, although they are more expensive (around £15 to £35), are the best option. Being solid, they are generally regarded as the most secure type of bicycle lock, providing maximum resistance to rust, picking and sawing.

Certain types of cycle locks offer an anti-theft guarantee, usually up to £500 against your bike being stolen. However, these guarantees often have strict claims limitations making the chance of a successful claim pretty slim.

Cycle alarms

The introduction of bike alarms is a fairly new development which may be worth considering in high-risk areas. Bike alarms work on the 'trembler' principle, going off when the bike is moved. They are battery-powered and are designed to be securely bolted to the bicycle frame. Some alarms are highly conspicuous, to deter a potential thief, while others are small and discreet, only being noticed when they actually go off. They are available from cycle shops and through specialist cycle magazines and cost around £25.

Security marking

You should mark your postcode on your bike frame and attach a coded cycle sticker to warn off thieves. This will help the police get it back to you if they find it. Many cycle dealers and police stations offer a free cycle-coding scheme – check with your local crime prevention officer for details.

Lock-up tips

- Always lock your bike when you leave it, even if you are just popping into a shop.
- Make sure you always lock your bike to something solid like a lamp-post or railings, with the lock passing through the frame and the rear of the front wheel. If you have quick-release wheels, take off the front wheel and lock it to the frame and back wheel using a second lock if necessary.
- Position the lock so that it can't be hammered against the ground or levered apart, and with the keyhole facing downwards.
- Always leave your bike in a well-lit, open space.
- Take lights and anything removable away with you.

Other schemes include Selectamark's 'Bicycle Security Register'. This involves chemically etching the bike frame with an individual coded number. Details of the bike are stored on a database, so stolen bikes that are recovered by the police can then be traced to their owner. The scheme is available through Halford stores and other specialist cycle dealers. It costs around £2 to £6 to have your bike security-marked and registered for five years. For more details contact Selectamark Security Systems.

Sophisticated marking systems aimed at more expensive bikes include the Datatag security device. This is fitted by a cycle dealer and involves placing a small microchip containing a unique ID number, inside the bicycle's frame. If the bike is stolen and later recovered, the police use a special scanner to read the data tag and identify the owner. For further details contact Nationwide Property Register. They offer a Datatag Protected Cycle Insurance Scheme – around £39 for a bike up to the value of £500 including the Datatag device.

Tip Take a good colour photo of your bike and keep a note of your bike's details including make and model, frame colour, frame number and size, where you bought it and any accessories or special features. The police will be able to match your bike to this if it is stolen and later recovered. You can get a 'recorded cycle' form from your local police station or cycle dealer.

CYCLE INSURANCE

After the lawn-mower, bikes are the next most popular item stolen from the garden so it's a good idea to get insurance for your bike. You may find that your household contents policy already offers some form of cover, which can work out cheaper than a specialist policy. But you'll need to check with your insurance company as to the cover available since it may not cover the bike when it's away from the house.

For more expensive bikes, it may be worth taking out a specific policy to suit your bike. Many bike clubs including the Cyclists' Touring Club, London Cycling Campaign, British Cycling Federation and British Mountain Bike Federation offer their own insurance schemes to members.

Premiums vary; for example, a £500 mountain bike costs from £65 to £100 to insure.

Security is also a consideration with insurance. The invincible cycle lock is yet to be invented, but most insurers insist that the bike be securely locked to an immovable object when it's left unattended. Some will not cover you if you leave your bike outside all night, or chained up outside work all day. Make sure your pattern of use is covered before taking out a policy.

Theft or damage are not the only problems faced by cyclists. If you cause an accident, or hit a pedestrian, the victims could sue you for damages. Most cycle insurance covers legal liability, but personal accident cover (for any injuries you suffer) is usually extra.

ENCOURAGE BICYCLE SECURITY

Why not join your fellow bicycle users in lobbying your local authority to provide proper cycle parking and other facilities for cyclists? You can get more information about the nearest cycle campaign in your area from the Cycle Campaign Network.

FURTHER HELP

Further information on crime prevention in general is provided in the Home Office booklet, *Your Practical Guide to Crime Prevention*. For a free copy, contact the Home Office (*see* Useful Addresses).

Chapter 8

Personal Security

You're hurrying home after dark and the streets are emptying. As you turn a corner you come face to face with a mugger. What would you do? Freeze? Hold on to your handbag tightly? Hit the mugger with your umbrella? You don't have to be a woman alone or an elderly person – personal attack is a crime we all dread.

Yet fortunately violent crimes such as being mugged or raped are relatively rare, although widespread media coverage of incidents has contributed to the fear, particularly among women. Statistics show that, in fact, 16- to 29-year-old men are at greatest risk of attack. Women are more likely to be in danger in their homes than on the street.

Despite the 180,000 assaults on women every year (according to Home Office estimates), violent crime is still comparatively rare. It accounts for a very small percentage of all recorded crime and should be put in perspective. The best way to minimise the risk of attack is by taking sensible precautions. Most people already do this as part of their everyday lives, often without realising it.

Self-defence and safety awareness classes may help you feel more secure and confident. Ask your local police or at your work if they have classes.

IN AN ATTACK

Ideally you should try to avoid getting into the situation in the first place. For example, stick to well-lit areas when walking alone at night. Be aware, trust your instincts.

The absolute priority if you are attacked, or think that you are in danger of attack, is to get away from the situation as quickly as you can. Shout, scream, let off a personal alarm, get as much attention as possible, and walk as fast as you can. Don't run immediately – you will be tense and are likely to fall over. Fight back only if you are being physically attacked.

The law says that you can 'use reasonable force' in self-defence. But it is an offence to carry anything that can be described as an offensive weapon, for example a knife or sharpened comb. (This obviously doesn't include things that you'd normally carry, such as hairspray or car keys.)

If the worst happens, you'll have very little thinking time so you must be able to trust your instinctive reactions. Spend some time considering what you would do in a tricky situation. One of the secrets of being safe is to think the unthinkable and plan how to react in advance.

PERSONAL ALARMS

A personal alarm can offer reassurance and help you feel safer when you are out on your own. It is intended to shock or disorientate an assailant

---

What to do in an attack

- Attract as much attention as possible: shout, scream and let off a personal alarm if you have one.
- Get away immediately. Don't wait to see what effect your shouting or the noise of the alarm is having. Your priority is to get away as fast as you can.
- Get to a safe area – a well-lit place with plenty of people, such as a shop, pub or garage. Even bang on the door of a house with lights on.
- If your handbag is snatched, let it go. If you hang on, you could get hurt. Remember your safety is more important than your property. (For this reason, keep a note of the emergency phone number to stop your credit cards, carry your house keys and a phonecard in your pocket, and keep emergency money on you in a moneybelt.)
- Try to remember what your attacker looked like and always call the police. Even if you were not actually assaulted, they still need to know – someone else may not be so lucky.

and give you time to get away. It may even attract attention – though you should not rely on this. The sound is as loud as a pneumatic drill and can be heard within a 400 m/¼ mile radius in rural areas and within 100–200 metres in town. Choose an alarm that is designed to continue sounding if it's dropped or falls to the ground.

Personal alarms are available from DIY stores or you could ask your local crime prevention officer where you can buy one. Some are available by mail order. There are two main types:

Electronic alarms, which are battery-powered, are usually triggered by pulling out a pin with a pull cord or by pressing or sliding a switch. They will sound continuously for at least half an hour or until you re-insert the pin.

Gas alarms work like a normal aerosol. When the cap is pressed, pressurised gas escapes, making a loud screech. The alarms can be locked-on so that they sound continuously, and are silenced by pulling the top off. Unfortunately, gas alarms can 'freeze up' and fall silent in very cold weather.

Using a personal alarm

- Remember to test your alarm periodically to check it is still working. With a gas alarm shake the can – if you can hear liquid rattling around then the alarm is serviceable. With an electronic alarm you should change the batteries regularly even if it hasn't been used, since old batteries will sometimes leak, damaging the alarm. Some electronic alarms have a test button.
- Carry the alarm in your hand so you can use it immediately to scare off an attacker. It's useless if it's buried at the bottom of your bag, or attached to your belt beneath a heavy coat. Don't wear an alarm with a long cord around your neck – the cord could be used to hurt you.
- Don't be afraid to use your alarm. Set it off immediately. Don't stop to think if it's necessary – trust your instincts.
- If you are attacked, hold the alarm up to the assailant, then throw it out of reach.

ON FOOT

When you are walking, carry your bag close to you with the clasp facing inwards. But don't carry it with the strap across your body – if you are mugged, you could be hurt if a knife is used to cut it off. Cover up expensive-looking jewellery.

If you think someone is following you, check by crossing the street – more than once if necessary – to see if he follows. If you are still worried, get to the nearest place where there are other people, such as a pub or shop, and call the police. Avoid using a phone box in the street, as the attacker could trap you inside.

If you regularly go walking or jogging (or cycling), try to vary your route and time. Stick to well-lit roads with pavements. On commons and parklands, keep to main footpaths and open spaces where you can see and be seen by other people – avoid wooded areas. If you wear a personal stereo, remember that you can't hear traffic or somebody approaching behind you.

Don't take short cuts through dark alleys, parks or waste ground. Don't hitchhike or take lifts from strangers. Walk facing the traffic so that a car cannot pull up behind you unnoticed.

If a car stops and you are threatened, scream and shout, and set off your personal attack alarm if you have one. Turn and walk away as quickly as you can – the car won't be able to turn nearly as easily. This will gain you vital seconds and make it more difficult for the car driver to follow. If you can, make a mental note of the registration number and a description of the car. Write down details as soon as possible afterwards.

TRAVELLING BY TAXI

If you're going to be out late, try to arrange a lift home or book a taxi. There are many reputable mini-cab or private hire-car companies but these must be booked in advance. In some cases the driver will carry identification. Always keep the number of a reliable firm handy. Avoid taxis that tout for business.

To make sure that the taxi that arrives is the one you ordered, ask for a description of the taxi – colour, make, etc. – when booking and check this when it arrives. If you gave your name when you booked, find out if the driver can tell you it before you get in. If in any doubt, *don't* get in.

Always sit behind the driver. If you feel uneasy, ask to be let out in a well-lit area where there are plenty of people. When you get home, ask the driver to wait until you are inside.

PUBLIC TRANSPORT

When travelling by public transport, try to stay away from isolated bus stops, especially after dark. In an empty bus, sit near the driver. On a train, sit in a compartment where there are several other people – ideally one which will be near the exit at your destination. Check to see where the emergency chain is. If travelling alone don't use closed carriages that are empty.

ON THE ROAD

Have your car serviced regularly by a reputable garage – a well-maintained car is less likely to break down. Join a breakdown recovery organisation. Many now offer priority treatment to lone women members.

Keep change and a phonecard in case you need to make a telephone call. If you frequently have to travel after dark, or if your job involves travel in your car, consider getting a mobile phone (*see* Mobile phones, page 61). Carry a torch. Also carry a spare can of petrol, jump-leads, a towrope, a fire extinguisher, a car jack and a warning triangle; make sure you know how to use them (*see* Safe-driving courses for women, page 59).

Before a long trip, check oil and windscreen-water levels and ensure you have enough petrol to reach your destination. Make sure your windscreen and headlights are clean. Plan your route if the journey is unfamiliar and stay on main roads if you can. Carry a road atlas. Before you leave, tell anyone you are planning to meet what time you think you will get there, and the route you are taking.

If someone tries to flag you down, drive on to a service station, or somewhere busy, and call the police. Do not pick up hitchhikers.

Keep doors locked when driving and keep any bag, mobile phone or valuables out of sight. If you have the window open, wind it down only a little. Don't wind it down far enough to allow someone to reach in while you are stopped in traffic.

If you think you are being followed, try to alert others by flashing your lights and sounding your horn. Make as much noise as possible. If you can, keep driving until you come to a busy place. Make a note of the registration number, colour and make of the car, then report the incident to the police.

Always lock your car even if you're only leaving it for a few minutes, for example when filling the car with petrol. Never leave the keys in the ignition. Don't forget that with central locking, if you undo one door all the others are unlocked including the boot. After dark, park in a well-lit, busy place (*see* Car parks, page 60). Look around before you get out.

Have your key ready when you return to your car and make sure there is no one in the car before you get in.

If you break down, find a telephone. On a motorway, try to coast to the nearest emergency telephone. The arrows on the marker posts indicate the direction of the nearest phone; phones are usually 1.6 km/1 mile apart. You don't need money to make the call and you will be automatically put through to the police motorway control centre, who will take your details.

Never attempt to carry out roadside repairs on a motorway. Always wait for professional help.

While on the hard shoulder or telephoning, keep a sharp look-out and don't accept lifts from strangers; wait for the police or breakdown service. Don't wait in the car – there is a high risk of an accident. Wait on the embankment nearby, with the front passenger door open. If someone approaches you or you feel threatened, lock yourself in the car and speak to them through a small gap in the window.

Safe-driving courses for women

If you are unsure what to do if you break down or if you hate driving alone at night, consider attending a safe-driving course. Being aware and knowing what to do in situations is the key to confident driving. It's lack

---

Self-education

'Smart Driving – Women at the Wheel' is an informative video offering practical advice for women motorists. Accompanying the video are laminated cards, designed to be kept in your car's glove compartment, which provide a quick reference to changing a tyre, breakdown procedures, safety checklist, etc. Priced around £13 the video is available by mail order from Smart Driving.

---

of knowledge that can put drivers, particularly women motorists, at risk. Research shows that women would feel far more confident behind the wheel if they knew the basics of car maintenance.

The AA, RAC and Britannia Rescue run safe-driving courses aimed at women. The courses provide practical advice and include basic car maintenance – how to check the oil and change a wheel, the procedure for breakdowns and accidents, and personal and in-car safety advice. The courses are available throughout the UK but operate on an ad hoc basis and are arranged locally to suit demand. Most require a minimum number of people. For further details contact the AA, RAC or Britannia Rescue.

Safe-driving courses or talks may also be run in conjunction with car dealers and manufacturers or your local police – check with your local crime prevention officer for details or look out for advertisements in your local paper.

Car parks

Car parks are not only a target for thieves but a source of fear for many people. If you need to park or return to your car after dark, look out for public car parks with the gold or silver 'Secured Car Parks Awards' logo, given by the police. The award sets high crime prevention standards of internal design and layout of the car park. It also indicates that the car park is well supervised, with restricted entry and exit points, and has good lighting and security cameras.

Only those that qualify are entitled to display

the 'Secured Car Parks' logo, and they are regularly inspected to ensure that standards are maintained.

To find out about Secured Car Parks in your area, contact your local crime prevention officer.

Tip Park as near to the main entrance or as close to the attendant's booth as you can. Reverse into a space so you can make a quick exit.

Mobile phones

Even if you feel you wouldn't use a mobile phone on a regular basis, there's no doubt that they offer peace of mind and personal security in the event of an accident or breakdown.

A recent RAC survey showed that 87 per cent of women motorists would feel safer with a mobile phone in the car to be able to summon help in an emergency without having to leave their car, children or belongings.

Breakdowns often occur at the worst possible moments – when you're in a hurry and miles from the nearest phone box or on an unknown and unlit country lane. Even if breakdowns occur on motorways, where an emergency phone is not very far away, you certainly won't want to leave your children alone in the car or take them with you along the hard shoulder.

Buying a mobile phone As mobile phones are becoming more affordable, many manufacturers are aiming them at the general public for

---

Drivers' alarms

If much of your driving takes you into built-up areas, a personal alarm fitted in your car is a good option. The alarm is fitted under the bonnet; when you press the panic button on the dashboard, a loud siren sounds, followed by a recording asking for help. Brands to look for include Waso's Help-Me Panic Alarm (£90 plus fitting) and Simba's Talking Guardian (£170 including fitting). The alarms must be professionally fitted and both companies can provide details of your nearest authorised installer.

Using a mobile phone

- Remember to charge the battery regularly – it takes only a few minutes.
- Don't leave a mobile phone on display. If you can't take it with you, lock the phone in the boot.
- Don't sit in stationary traffic talking on the phone with your window open. If you need to use the phone in this situation, make sure all your windows are closed and doors are locked.
- Make a note of the phone's identity number and mark your postcode on the handset with an ultraviolet marker pen. That way, if it's stolen and later recovered by the police it can be returned to you.
- Get insurance cover. Insurance will often be offered as part of the package; if not, it costs around £50 per year. (Some household contents policies will cover it, so check with your insurance company first.)
- If you intend to use the phone in your car, buy a car kit so you can make calls without taking your hands off the steering wheel, which is illegal. They usually cost around £200 extra.
- If you use a mobile phone to contact the emergency services or a breakdown organisation when you break down, make sure you know your exact location, especially on a motorway.

---

use in emergencies. For the first time, there is a wide range available at less than £150, making mobile phones a more viable security option.

If you decide to buy a mobile phone, go to a reputable dealer or retailer who can advise you on which network and what type of phone to choose. If you prefer a one-stop shop, The Carphone Warehouse has the networks under one roof and can provide information if needed – call free on 0800 424800.

Special mobile phones

AA Callsafe is a special in-car portable phone which uses Vodafone's network to provide access to emergency services or the AA. Callsafe is powered from the car's battery via the cigarette lighter socket or an optional battery pack. A one-off connection fee is about £25, handset £150, and quarterly line rental £26. Call the AA free on 0500 161718 for further details.

Ford Call uses the cellnet network. Ford is offering a mobile phone and line connection free of charge with every new Ford car sold. The phone features an emergency help button which automatically connects the caller to the 24-hour RAC/Ford Control Centre. Women driving alone, especially at night, will be given priority. The monthly line rental starts from around £10. Further information is available from your local Ford dealer or call free on 0800 111222.

MALICIOUS PHONE CALLS

A harassing or malicious phone caller can make you feel unpleasantly vulnerable in your own home. British Telecom receives over 200,000 requests for help each year from people getting malicious calls. If you receive an abusive or threatening call:

- Don't give your name or phone number. Say nothing, walk away from the phone and gently hang up without saying anything after a few minutes – don't listen to hear if the caller is still there.
- If the calls continue, tell the police and the operator and keep a record of each phone call. This may help the authorities trace the caller.

Telephone tips

- When you answer the phone, simply say 'hello' – don't give your number. If the caller claims to have a wrong number, ask him or her to say the number they require. Never reveal any information about yourself to a stranger and never say you are alone in the house.
- Never give your address over the phone unless you are absolutely sure you know the caller.
- Don't enter into any conversation with a malicious caller.
- Use only your surname and initials in the telephone directory. That way a stranger won't know whether a man or a woman lives there.

- The operator can intercept all your calls (usually for about two weeks) at no extra charge. If necessary, your telephone number can be changed.
- 'Caller display' allows you to see the number of the person calling before answering the phone. Even if malicious callers use the 141 withhold code, BT can trace callers at police request.
- BT can organise Malicious Call Identification free of charge but only as part of a police investigation.
- British Telecom offer an advice service and leaflet on how to deal with malicious callers: call free on 0800 666700, where a recorded message will advise you. For personal advice, contact BT's Malicious Calls Bureau free on 0800 661441.

FURTHER HELP

The police offer free talks, pamphlets and videos on personal security – contact your local crime prevention officer for details. For further information on personal security, contact the Suzy Lamplugh Trust.

Victim Support is a national charity which offers free and confidential advice and emotional support to crime victims. Contact them during office hours (*see* Useful Addresses).

Chapter 9

Child Security

Ask any mother what her greatest fears are for her children's safety and it's likely that attack and abduction will be top of the list.

However, it must be said that the risk of abduction or murder is relatively rare in the UK. On average, every year seven children (which includes teenagers up to 16 years) are murdered and 750 assaulted by a stranger. The biggest danger to children, by far, is being involved in a road traffic accident. In 1992, over 44,000 children were injured on the roads (more than 300 of them fatally). Fire and drowning are the next most common causes of accidental death (in the under-14-year-olds). Yet, according to a recent survey, 22 per cent of parents put attack top of the list of threats to our children – ahead of road accidents and drugs.

Set against this background, sales of products designed to safeguard children are booming, ranging from child harnesses to sophisticated personal alarms. Some shopping centres are even considering handing out electronic tagging devices for parents and children to use while on the premises. If the child wanders out of sight, the adult can use a handset to activate an audible alarm on the child's device. If this doesn't locate the child, security staff will track the child on a computer screen. This device is still under trial but, hopefully, will be available in the near future.

CHILDREN'S SECURITY DEVICES

It's on family days out or during a shopping trip that a child is most likely to get separated from his or her parents. Personal security devices can give reassurance, but they are not foolproof. They may give parents a false sense of security, and reinforce the idea to the child that something could go wrong. It must be remembered that these devices are no substitute for teaching a child about personal safety, so think carefully before using one.

Electronic reins

With this device, the child wears a radio receiver unit, and the parent a transmitter. If the child goes outside a pre-set range, the alarm will sound on the parent's unit. Prices vary from £25 to £60.

Personal alarms

There are numerous gas- and battery-operated alarms (primarily designed for women), costing as little as £3 (*see* personal alarms, page 56). Only give one to your child if you feel he or she is responsible enough to use it in a crisis; they must understand that it will not necessarily bring help, just put

---

Safety sense

There is no substitute for teaching your child about safety and it's never too early to start.

- Start teaching your child the rudiments of road sense and personal safety as soon as he or she is able to walk. And try to do it in a fun and constructive manner.
- Teach your child never to talk to strangers when they are not with an adult, and never to get into a stranger's car.
- Teach your child to yell, run and tell if he or she is accosted by a stranger. It is important to practise this with your children (without being alarming), so that they get used to the idea of frightening off an adult.
- When you go out shopping or attend a large, crowded event, arrange a meeting point with your child in case you get separated. If you haven't done this, always go back to the last place you saw the child.
- With small children, maintain some kind of physical contact, whether it's holding hands or using child reins.
- Teach your child to find someone in uniform, such as an assistant behind a shop counter or a police officer, or a mum with young children of her own, if they suddenly find themselves in trouble.
- From a very early age most children can remember their surname. This is more helpful over a tannoy than a description such as 'a young girl in a red dress'.

the assailant off for a few seconds. It might be useful, for instance, for a child on a paper round. But the child shouldn't be encouraged to rely on it – practical safety advice is more important. If you're unsure about giving your child a particular security device, talk it over with your local crime prevention officer.

Identity labels

These are a simple, sensible precaution designed to help identify a child in an emergency. The labels would be useful 'extra insurance' for very young children who may panic and not be able to remember their complete name in a crisis. To be properly effective, labels should be put in every pair of the child's shoes where they are discreet and not immediately obvious.

Durable and waterproof labels printed with the child's name and postcode are available from Childcheck, £5 for a pack of 20.

SAFETY AND CRIME PREVENTION COURSES

There are now a number of schemes and courses to help children learn about potential dangers in an imaginative, safe and controlled way. The Junior Citizen Scheme (in London) and Crucial Crew (outside London) help 9- to 11-year-olds cope with all kinds of everyday dangers including bike security, road safety, stranger danger, safety and security in the home. These courses usually take place in schools during term time. Contact Crime Concern for courses outside London or New Scotland Yard – Community Affairs Branch – for details of your nearest London-based scheme.

FURTHER HELP

If you would like further information about how to teach your child practical steps to stay safe, send a large, stamped, self-addressed envelope to Kidscape, a charity which campaigns for children's safety (*see* Useful Addresses).

Chapter 10

Safety Throughout the Home

Every household is different. Take a good look at your home, room by room, and carry out a safety audit to see where the possible hazards lie.

KITCHEN

If you are planning a new kitchen, it's easy to get caught up with the overall look and the smart new appliances you would like to include but don't forget to consider how practical and safe it will be. You'll need to think about the layout, design and positioning of appliances carefully.

If, on the other hand, you have inherited a kitchen, you may also be taking on a lot of potential problem areas. It is important to be aware of badly planned/fitted kitchens, particularly if you have small children around. Ask yourself:

- Is the lighting adequate over the work surfaces?
- Are the plug sockets well positioned or will flexes trail near the sink or cooker?
- Are the edges of worktops or corners of tables sharp? You may need to consider using corner protectors.
- Is the kitchen ventilated adequately? Proper ventilation is vital, especially if you have gas appliances in the kitchen and to provide a clean, airy environment.

- Are there unhygienic gaps in tiles on work surfaces? Crevices can harbour germs, so seal with waterproof sealant.
- Is there safe storage of hazardous cleaning chemicals and medicines?
- Do you have glass-fronted doors that would be safer with laminated glass?
- How even and ruck-free is the flooring? Torn lino or tiles that are not properly stuck down are a hazard.
- Have you inherited electrical appliances with unknown histories? Get them serviced.
- Have the previous owners installed the units themselves? Check how secure they are, especially wall units.
- How strong are the shelves? They should be capable of supporting the equivalent of a 2 kg/4½ lb pack of sugar throughout their length. Put heavy and fragile items in a low but secure position, and don't overload shelves. Make sure the shelves have shelf retainers to prevent them tipping forward if a heavy weight is placed at the front.

KITCHEN HAZARDS

We use a variety of household appliances every day and often neglect to treat them with the respect they deserve. Have them serviced regularly to ensure they are safe and working properly.

If you have children, look for child-safety features when buying new appliances. These include child locks on washing machines and tumble dryers, and cool-touch doors on cookers.

Cooker
- Don't leave saucepans unattended.
- Try to get into the habit of using the pan that best fits the size of hob ring available. If possible, use the rings at the back of the hob and remember to turn the handles inward (so that they don't overhang the edge of the cooker or get dangerously hot over another hob ring).
- When using a deep-fat frying pan, never fill it more than one third full with oil or two-thirds full when the food has been added.

- When cleaning, switch the cooker off at the wall panel.
- Don't be tempted to line any part of the cooker with kitchen foil to keep it clean – fat from foods may catch fire.

Kettle

- If you have a corded kettle, buy a curly cord or check to see if you can wind the flex underneath so that the kettle cannot be sited too near the front of the work surface.
- Switch off and unplug at the wall socket before you fill or pour it. Fill with enough water to cover the element completely.
- If buying new, opt for a cordless kettle and site the power base near the back of the work surface.

Toaster

- It's tempting to fish around with a knife to loosen bread caught inside the toaster. Never do this without switching off and unplugging first, otherwise you may get an electric shock. Allow the toaster to cool, and only then remove the bread, with a wooden spatula. (If buying a new toaster, look for one with an extra lift facility for easier access.)
- Do not disturb the heat elements. Never poke about with a fork or similar metal object or you are likely to break them.
- Clean the toaster regularly to remove loose breadcrumbs, which can pose a fire risk. Follow the manufacturer's instructions. Many models now have removable crumb trays.

Iron

- Always fill steam irons before you plug them in. Make sure the iron base is dry before you use it.
- Fit a flex holder to the ironing board. This will keep the flex away from the edge of the ironing board and help prevent it from fraying.
- Never use an iron with a worn flex. The majority of new irons have plastic coated flexes which are more durable.
- Never wrap the flex around a hot iron.
- When ironing, always stand the iron on its heel. Never leave an iron

face down.
- If you are worried about accidentally leaving the iron on after use, buy a model that automatically switches itself off after a few seconds if left in the ironing position.

Kitchen knives
- Don't keep sharp knives loose in the utensil drawer – use a knife block at the back of the work surface or wall rack (but don't overload it).
- Knives should be washed separately from the rest of the cutlery to avoid bad cuts from hidden knives in soapy water. (The same applies to food processor blades.)
- Sharpen knives regularly. A sharp knife is much safer than a blunt knife.
- Never use knives with wet hands.

Medicines and household chemicals
- Always lock all medicines and chemicals away out of children's reach in a high cupboard, preferably in the kitchen where there are always more adults around than in a bathroom.
- Try to buy cleaning products and medicines in child-resistant containers.
- Never transfer cleaning liquids to other containers such as squash bottles, in case children mistakenly think they are drinks.
- Don't take labels off.
- Always read instructions and warnings carefully.
- Never mix products as they may give off toxic fumes. Only dilute them if the label clearly states it is safe to do so.
- If you have medicine left over, don't keep it or throw it in the dustbin. Take it back to the pharmacist so it can be destroyed.

Household cleaning agents
Remember that some household cleaning products are potentially dangerous substances. Be sure you know for what purpose the product is intended and read the information and warning messages carefully.

Caustic soda (sodium hydroxide) This is a very strong alkali. If using caustic soda crystals, remember they are corrosive and can burn the skin so it's important to follow all the safety instructions. Wear rubber gloves and avoid inhaling fumes. Use only in a well-ventilated room. If you are overcome by fumes, get to an open window as quickly as possible. For accidental splashes on the skin, rinse the affected area well under a running cold water tap.

Chlorine bleach (sodium hypochlorite) Always store bleach in a safe place. Don't be tempted to add it to any other household chemicals or proprietary cleaners to speed things up, as it may then give off toxic gases which can be extremely dangerous. Wear rubber gloves.

If you spill any on your skin, wash the affected area immediately with plenty of cold water. If any is accidentally swallowed, drink plenty of water followed by plenty of milk then contact your doctor immediately.

Solvents (includes acetone and turpentine) Keep all grease solvents well away from flames and sparks. Avoid inhaling fumes and vapours, and always work in a well-ventilated room. Avoid prolonged contact with the skin as the solvent may cause it to feel dry. Keep solvents well out of reach of children.

Tip If you are worried about children and solvent abuse contact the charity Re-Solv for advice.

Ammonia This is a poison. Don't allow it to be taken internally, and never open the bottle caps to smell the contents. Avoid contact with the eyes, skin and clothing. If ammonia is swallowed, make the person drink plenty of cold water, then contact your doctor immediately. Wear rubber gloves, always use it in a well-ventilated room and store the bottle in a cool, dark and safe place.

BATHROOM

Many accidents take place in the bathroom. Inevitably, in an area where you are dealing with water, there are a number of potential dangers.

Baths, showers and sinks

Always use non-slip bath mats in the bath. (For awkward shapes, try Slipsafe spray inside baths or shower trays; it will bond to most surfaces.) Consider fitting bath grips for elderly members of the family to assist them in getting in or out of the bath.

Make sure the areas around your bath, shower tray and sink are properly sealed with bath sealant. This can be a breeding ground for germs in a hot, wet environment, and the sealant will prevent water damage to the room below and also prevent wet rot.

Install bath shower screens or curtains to help prevent water from escaping on to the bathroom floor.

Electricity

There should be no electrical plugs in the bathroom but if you live in an old house which has not been rewired, watch for this and get in an electrician to advise you. All lights should be on pull-cords not switches.

Make sure the shaver socket is situated well out of reach of children. Radiant heaters, towel rails and mirror lights must be fixed firmly to the wall. They should have permanent wiring (which means sockets) and pull-cord switches. Don't fix them above the bath or near a shower. Heaters must be out of reach of people using the bath, and heaters with metal frames must be securely earthed and bonded to other metalwork in the bathroom. Have all work carried out by a qualified electrician.

Never use a portable electric fire, hairdryer or other electrical equipment in the bathroom.

Hot water

All shower water-heaters should have anti-scald thermal cut-outs. If buying new, opt for thermostatic models that are designed to stabilise any temperature changes whilst you're under the shower. Mechanical shower mixers are less expensive but do not offer the same degree of temperature control and safety.

If you have a gas water-heater in the bathroom, there should be adequate ventilation at all times.

- Hot-water thermostats should be set at 54°C/129°F.
- Ensure that the radiators and towel rails are kept at a safe temperature
- When filling the bath, start with cold water and then add hot water

General safety

Take care not to leave medicines, cosmetics, household cleaners, razors and razor blades within reach of children.

Never use loose rugs in bathrooms. All rugs should have safety grips.

LIVING ROOM, STAIRS AND HALLWAY

Heating

Never hang things over a convector heater or storage heater. Portable heaters can start a fire if misused. Make sure the heater has a permanent safety guard, is used only in a well-ventilated area and is clean and well maintained. Always turn it off before you go to bed. Electric heaters should carry the British Electrotechnical Approvals Board (BEAB) approval mark. Portable gas heaters should carry the BSI Kitemark.

If you have any heaters on time switches, keep them well clear of curtains and furnishings. Never fit time-switched or delay controls to an electric fire.

Open fires cause 1,400 fires each year. Use a spark-guard over the fire when you are not there to keep an eye on it. Don't forget to have the chimney swept at least once a year even if you use smokeless fuel. Don't place mirrors over fireplaces: it encourages people to stand too close to them.

TV and stereo

Switch off when you are not using the TV and stereo and take the mains plug out of the supply socket. Never try to repair them yourself: call in a specialist.

Lighting

Switch off light fittings and allow the bulbs to cool before removing them. To avoid causing a fire, do not use higher-wattage bulbs than the makers recommend on shades and fittings.

Flooring and stairs

Stick down loose tiles and sheet vinyl. Neaten off frayed carpet edges.

Don't polish floors under loose rugs or carpets or place rugs at the base of stairs. Rugs can be fitted with adhesive underlay. This is available from specialist carpet retailers, or contact the British Carpet Manufacturers' Association for stockists.

Ensure stair rods are securely fixed and the carpet is not loose. Never leave objects on the stairs. Check that banisters and railings are firm.

Keep stairs and halls well lit. Install two-way light switches so you can switch on the light at the top or bottom of the stairway.

Windows

Each year around 27,000 people in Britain are injured by glass in their homes. It may be worth considering safety-glazing fully glazed doors, door side panels, wet areas (e.g. shower screens), low-level glazing and glass in furniture – especially if you have young children.

Glass in any window, whether it is double-glazed or not, can be difficult to break in the event of an emergency. It is important to have at least one window in every room which can be opened from the inside, and which is wide enough to be used as an emergency exit. For windows with locks, always make sure that the key to the window is kept in a safe place (out of reach of children), and that everyone in the family knows where it is kept.

BEDROOMS

Electric blankets

Each year British fire brigades are called to some 1,500 fires caused by electric blankets. More than 20 people are killed and 250 injured in these fires. Only use electric blankets which conform to the BEAB (British Electrotechnical Approvals Board) safety mark; BS 3999, Part 6, or BS EN 60967 and always follow the manufacturer's instructions.

Not all electric blankets can be left on all night: check your instructions.

Over-blankets are designed to be tucked in at the sides and bottom of the bed, without any of the heated area being folded under.

Fire safety and fabrics

One in six house fires starts on upholstery furnishings, accounting for 30 per cent of all deaths and injuries. When buying upholstered furniture (new or second-hand) check it conforms to the 1988 Furniture and Furnishings Fire Safety Regulations. This means it's made from flame-retardant fabric that won't catch fire so easily and, if it did ignite, it will burn more slowly. If your upholstered furniture and bedding were made before the 1988 fire safety regulations, consider improving their resistance to fire.

- If you are making loose covers for a sofa or armchair, look for match-resistant fabric (ask the advice of your fabric supplier). If you're using a fabric that can't easily be treated for flame-retardancy (such as glazed chintz and silks), use a flame-retardant barrier fabric underneath.
- If you are having furniture reupholstered, replacement covers and any material supplied in the course of a reupholstering service must now meet the requirements of the 1988 Furniture and Furnishings Fire Safety Regulations. For further safety you could also have the filling replaced with a flame-retardant one or, at least, use a flame-retardant barrier fabric fitted between the new cover and the existing filling material to help protect the old fillings in the event of a fire.
- Flame-retardant sprays can be applied to fabrics, carpets and upholstery such as Cope & Timmins's Fire Screen (about £8 for 1 litre/1¾ pints). They may not always be as effective as flame-resistant treatments that are applied by a factory process. Check that the spray is suitable for the fabric on your furniture and follow the manufacturer's instructions carefully. Be warned: spray treatments that are not water-resistant will simply wash out if liquids such as tea are spilt on the treated fabric.
- Alternatively, you can have fabric treated for flame-retardancy by a dry cleaner or *in situ* by a carpet/upholstery cleaning company.

Which safety glass?

There are various types of safety glass, so for guidance go to an expert: a member of the Glass and Glazing Federation. Prices vary, but you can expect to pay up to twice as much as for ordinary glass. Use glazing materials that meet BS 6206.

Toughened glass is made by heating ordinary glass to a high temperature and following this with rapid cooling. It's up to five times stronger than ordinary glass so is difficult to break. When it does, it shatters into thousands of relatively harmless pieces, rather like a car windscreen.

Laminated glass is made from two or more sheets of ordinary glass with a tough layer of plastic in between. On impact the glass will break but the pieces will remain together on the plastic interlayer, so minimising any injuries.

Adhesive plastic safety film can be applied to one side of ordinary glass to hold the pieces together if the glass breaks. Follow the manufacturer's instructions carefully.

Check blankets regularly for wear, have them serviced every two to three years, and never buy one second-hand as there is no safety guarantee.

Hairdryers

Do not wrap the flex around the handle of a hairdryer when you have finished with it. Unplug it when not in use. Regularly clean the filter of hair and dust. Many filters are detachable for easier cleaning.

Smoking

Never smoke in bed due to the risk of fire. Keep matches and lighters out of the reach of children.

Chapter 11

Child-proofing Your Home

What may seem like a perfectly safe home can suddenly become an assault course of potential hazards once there is a child in the house. If you have young children then you've probably spotted most of the danger zones already but there may be some which still lurk undetected. Pinpointing the hazards is more difficult when your home is only occasionally invaded by small children.

Each year in Britain, one in five children under the age of 15 is taken to hospital after an accident in or around the home. Not surprisingly, younger children are far more likely to have an accident at home than older children, with children under the age of four being particularly at risk.

Realistically, no home can be totally child-proof. However, there is plenty you can do to prevent really serious accidents happening to children. Here are some of the ways you can make a child's environment safer. Don't worry if you are not able to implement all the measures outlined in this chapter – concentrate on those that are most applicable to your children, bearing in mind their age and inclinations.

It is important not to be negative about safety or to allow it to dominate your life by thinking all the time in terms of stair gates, fire-guards or cooker guards. Try not to be over-protective or to keep a child safe by making it afraid of things.

STAIRS

Never allow your child to play on or around the stairs. There's little to beat the challenge of climbing the stairs. Barriers or gates (from around £12) should be fitted at both the top and bottom of the staircase. Look for those that conform to BS 4125 as this ensures that the spacing between the bars and the gap between the lower edge and the floor are much too small for a youngster to wriggle his or her head through.

Tip   Buy a gate that can be opened easily with one hand.

Board up horizontal balcony rails so they cannot be used as a ladder. Fix loose carpets and check that the carpet tacks have not worked their way through worn patches.

Keep stairs and halls well lit. Fit a dimmer switch on the landing light, to keep the light on low through the night in case children want to go to the toilet.

WINDOWS

Small children love climbing up to peer out of windows but, once up there, it is all too easy for them to topple out. Don't put anything that a child can climb on to near a window.

Vertical window bars may save a toddler's life but do make sure they can be removed quickly in the event of a fire. Less conspicuous are window limiters which only allow the window to be opened a little way – enough to allow fresh air in but not sufficient for a toddler to get out.

Keep sash windows locked at the bottom.

Check that patio doors, shower screens, glass tables and conservatory glazing are all made from safety glass. If they are, the glass will be marked with the BS 6206 or BSI Kitemark. If not, replace them with laminated or toughened glass conforming to BS 6206, or at least cover them with safety film. (*See* Which safety glass?, page 77.)

IN THE KITCHEN

Young children are at risk of serious injury from hot liquids and cooking fat. Every year around 30,000 children go to hospital with scalds.

Keep the kettle at the back of the work surface, out of the reach of toddlers, and with the lead as short as is practical. Alternatively, buy a coiled flex for your kettle, keep it at the back of the work surface or use a kettle guard. (This screws to the wall at the back of the work surface and costs about £5.)

Knives and utensils must always be locked away or stored well out of reach.

Simple child-proof locks (£2–£4) should be fitted to kitchen cupboards and drawers and medicine cabinets. Freezer and fridge locks are also available. From DIY and department stores or leading nursery retail outlets such as Mothercare.

Try to cook on the back rings of the hob, and always remember to point saucepan handles inwards or towards the rear. Use a cooker guard (£12–£15) to stop toddlers pulling pans off the hob. Cooker guards are available from DIY and department stores or leading nursery retail outlets.

An oven built in at eye-level ensures that at least one hot area is out of reach of children. If you're buying a new oven, look for a model with a cool-touch door.

Doors on washing machines, dishwashers and tumble dryers should be kept closed. Don't forget that the doors on washer-dryers can get very hot during use unless they're double-insulated. If they are not, some models may have optional door guards.

Never store soft drinks and alcohol in the same, low-level cupboard.

Choose bottles with child-resistant lids where possible. Keep household cleaners and aerosol cans well out of reach.

First aid tip If a child is scalded, run cold water over the scald right away. Don't stop to remove clothing. Then get medical help for anything but the smallest accident.

IN THE LIVING ROOM

Make sure bookcases and wall units are well secured and cannot be pulled over when used as climbing frames.

Guards should be fitted to all fires and heaters: look for BS 6539 on guards for open fires; and BS1945 on guards for electric, gas and paraffin heaters. Check too that there's at least 20 cm (8 in) between the heat source and the guard, otherwise the guard will become dangerously hot.

Don't place things on the mantelpiece which might encourage a child to climb up and investigate.

Always extinguish cigarettes properly and empty ashtrays. Keep cigarettes, lighters and matches out of reach and lock alcohol away.

Consider fitting door-slam protectors to stop fingers being crushed.

Check if house-plants are poisonous or whether they cause allergies.

Consider fixing ornaments and movable objects in position with sticky pads or other fixings.

Play pens are advisable for toddlers for those occasions when you simply can't be in two places at once. Buy one made to BS 4863.

IN THE BATHROOM

Try to ensure that the floor covering is water-resistant without being slippery and that any rugs have a non-slip backing. In the bath itself, a non-slip rubber bath mat will help prevent the child from sliding under the water. Babies can drown in only a few inches of water so never leave them alone in the bath – even for a moment.

Ensure that the child cannot reach the lock on the bathroom or toilet door, in case they lock themselves in. Move locks if necessary.

Baths should always be filled with cold water before hot. Mix the water well and test the temperature with your elbow before you put a baby in.

If bathing a baby in a baby bath, check that the stand for the bath is solid and fits the bath well. If the bath is part of a changing unit, make sure that the mat or cover lifts off or slides away completely, and cannot drop down on to your baby while he or she is in the bath. Once a child can stand unaided, stop using the baby bath on a stand. Either use an adult bath or put the baby bath inside the adult bath.

For toddlers who delight in flushing toys, shoes, etc., down the loo you can buy a lid lock.

IN THE BEDROOM

Non-toxic nursery paint (available from specialist paint and hardware stores) should be used for children's rooms and furniture. Check that it complies to BS 5665.

Encourage children to be tidy and put their toys away after use, to prevent someone from tripping and falling over objects on the floor.

Check that the wardrobe doors can be opened from the inside in case your child gets stuck and that wardrobes and chests of drawers are secured to the wall so that they cannot be pulled over.

Don't leave medicines (including the contraceptive pill), cosmetics, nail scissors, etc., within a small child's reach.

Changing units Make sure the unit is stable when the drawers and cupboard are both open and closed. Make sure you can reach everything you need without leaving your baby alone on the unit.

Nappy buckets Keep nappy-sanitising powder out of reach. Your baby could swallow it and burn his mouth and throat. Keep nappy buckets out of the way. A child could drown in a full bucket or use the bucket as a step for climbing and reaching hazards.

Cribs Make sure the stand for the crib is firm and that swinging cribs can be locked into a resting position.

Moses baskets Make sure the fabric lining is stitched firmly into place and that there are no loose folds which could smother your baby.

Cots and cot beds Always put the side up when the baby is in the cot. Drop the mattress base to the lowest position as soon as your baby can sit himself up. Don't put the cot near curtains or anything that might help your baby climb out. Remove any toys from across the cot once your baby can move about; it could hurt itself. As soon as your baby starts trying to climb out of the cot, either switch to a bed or leave the drop side down. Keep the bedroom door closed or put a gate across it so that he or she cannot get out of the room at night.

First grown-up bed

If the child has just graduated to his or her first grown-up bed, consider

---

Reduce the risk of cot death

- Lay your baby down to sleep on either its back or side. Only lay it on its tummy if your doctor advises it. Once your baby is able to roll over on its own, there's no reason to stop it from sleeping in the position it prefers.
- Put your baby near the head of the cot to ensure it cannot become completely covered by the bedclothes.
- Don't smoke, and avoid smoky atmospheres.
- Don't let your baby get too hot. Babies don't need hot rooms – around 18°C/65°F is ideal.
- Don't use a hot water bottle or a sheepskin.
- If you think your baby is unwell, contact your doctor.
- For further information on cot death, contact either the Foundation for the Study of Infant Deaths (FSID) or the Cot Death Society.

---

using a bed guard to stop them falling out. (This is a tubular frame with a soft mesh infill. It is held in place with swivel arms which slide beneath the mattress and attach to the opposite side of the bed.)

Don't put under-fives in the top deck of a bunk bed and move beds and other furniture away from windows to stop children from climbing on windowsills and falling out.

ELECTRICAL APPLIANCES

Put safety socket covers on unused electrical sockets to keep prying little fingers and sharp objects away. Put furniture in front of electric sockets.

Use a residual current device (RCD) in areas in which your children live and play. It will automatically cut off the power in a fraction of a second, before your child receives a serious shock. It plugs into the wall socket, and the appliance is plugged into it.

Make the TV and stereo strictly out-of-bounds. You can buy video shields (£7) to stop little fingers playing with buttons and altering the programming, or video locks (£5) which fit across the cassette slot to prevent children from pushing toys into the machine. Some video recorders have child-locks incorporated. Video shields and locks are available from DIY and department stores or leading nursery retail outlets such as Mothercare and Early Learning.

Look out for trailing flexes and clip them out of harm's way. Never leave a lamp without a bulb.

> **Help with safety equipment**
>
> If you can't afford to buy items such as stair gates, car seats or fire-guards, speak to your health visitor, GP or the Social Services about loan schemes in your area.

PLAY EQUIPMENT

Check that outdoor play equipment is sturdy and well-maintained.

Paddling pools must always be emptied and ponds always covered when children are around. If you have a garden pond, fence it or, better still, drain it.

Climbing frames or swings should be placed on a grassy surface or on ground covered with bark chippings.

Sand pits should always be covered when not in use to stop dogs or cats fouling them.

TOY SAFETY

Children are spoilt for choice with the variety of toys and games available today. Choosing and using toys wisely is an essential part of helping your child get the most out of toys and games.

We all expect toys to be extra-safe. After all, they are for children. But every year, especially at Christmas time, we read about dangerous toys such as teddy bears that catch fire or dolls with nasty spikes and of the injuries suffered by children.

Fortunately, unsafe toys are rare. Most toys on the British market are carefully made and safe to play with. There are a number of organisations working to make sure safety standards are maintained, from the European Commission and the British Government to Trading Standards Officers, safety experts and the manufacturers themselves.

Always buy toys from a reputable shop, ideally one that is a member of the British Association of Toy Retailers (BATR). Look for their logo in the shop window or contact the BATR for details of your nearest toy shop member. You are more likely to get useful help and advice if you go to a specialist toy shop, the toy department of a large department store or the toy section of a major chain. Don't be tempted to buy cheap imitations of popular toys. These may seem good value but could turn out to be of inferior quality. Avoid buying second-hand toys from car boot sales and other fund-raising events; you have no guarantee of their safety.

When buying toys, it's important to take time and choose with care. Look out for the following:

The Lion Mark

This is a symbol of safety and quality, backed by a code of practice, developed by the British Toy & Hobby Association (BTHA) who represent 90 per cent of the British toy market. Only members of the association may apply for a licence to display the Lion Mark.

Toys bearing the Lion Mark have been manufactured to the high quality of materials and design required by the British Standard BS 5665/EN71. (The standard covers the mechanical and physical properties of toys, their flammability, toxicity of paints and dyes, etc.) The mark is also used by 'Approved Lion Mark Retailer' shops – a scheme developed by the British Toy & Hobby Association and British Association of Toy Retailers to indicate that all toys sold in that shop conform to the Lion Mark standard. Look for the special sign displayed in the shop window.

The CE mark

There has been much confusion about the CE mark. The CE mark is *not* a consumer mark. It is a mark of conformity aimed at assisting the free movement of goods within the European Community. It merely represents the manufacturer's claim that the toy is made in accordance with the essential requirements of the European Toy Safety Directive. All

---

Batteries

When changing batteries, always replace the whole set at the same time, taking care to insert the batteries correctly and not to mix old and new batteries or different types. Both can result in leakage, fire or, in extreme cases, an explosion. Don't allow young children to change batteries.

If toys are not played with for longer than a week, remove the batteries to avoid damage from corrosion. Always follow the manufacturer's recommendations and instructions.

Remember, small batteries, such as those used in watches and some calculators, are a danger to children, particularly very young children, who may choke on them or even swallow them completely. Never leave any batteries lying around.

---

toys must carry this mark. Therefore, when looking for a mark of safety and quality, you should always look for the Lion Mark.

Age guidelines

Messages such as 'recommended for children aged 3–4 years' are discretionary guidelines. They are the manufacturer's recommendation as to the suitability of the toy for a particular age group and can help you decide if the toy will be fun for your child to play with.

Small parts and age warnings

A safety message such as 'not suitable for children under 36 months' is not an age guideline, but refers to the toy's safety. It means that the toy

---

Dangerous toys

Although they are illegal, unsafe toys can still be found on sale. If you discover a dangerous toy, report it to your local Trading Standards Officer. If the toy does not comply with safety standards, it can be removed from the shelves and the sellers, distributors and manufacturers prosecuted.

---

has some element that could be potentially harmful to a small child, such as small parts or felt-tip pens. It should therefore be taken seriously.

Remember that some toys for older children are dangerous for babies or toddlers so if you have children of several ages, try and keep their toys separate.

Look out for a new pictorial symbol which is appearing on toys from 1995. It clearly indicates if a toy is unsuitable for a child under three years of age.

FURTHER HELP

For more information on toy safety contact either the National Toy Council or the British Toy & Hobby Association (BTHA). For further information on child safety in general, contact the Child Accident Prevention Trust (*see* Useful Addresses).

Safe toy buying

- Check toys in the shop. Insist on seeing an unwrapped sample.
- Check soft toys for sturdy, well-sewn seams. Make sure there are no sharp ends inside them and that eyes and noses are securely fastened and cannot be bitten off or pulled off by inquisitive little fingers.
- Check toys for sharp points or rough edges.
- Make sure that toys are painted with lead-free paint.
- Avoid items containing liquid that a child could drink if the toy broke.
- Avoid cheap toys made in the Far East.
- Remove all dangerous packaging before wrapping a toy for a child.
- For handmade toys, choose fabric or fur that is flame-retardant, or at least use a flame-retardant barrier fabric under the cover fabric. Beware of those sold at craft fairs.
- Regularly check your children's toys for safety. If the toy cannot be repaired properly, throw it away.

Chapter 12

Services

Most of us worry, at one time or another, whether we've unplugged the iron or switched off the gas cooker before going out. But few people are aware of the full dangers from the domestic services that we take so much for granted.

Protecting yourself, your family and your home is simple if you use care and common sense. Fitting smoke alarms and ensuring that appliances and central heating systems are regularly serviced are just some of the ways you can help.

Make sure that all members of the family know the location of stopcocks, fuse-boxes, the mains power switch, the gas mains and what possible exit routes to use in the event of a fire.

GAS

Never carry out any DIY repairs to gas pipes, fittings or appliances. Have all gas appliances professionally installed and serviced regularly by a CORGI-registered gas installer (Council for Registered Gas Installers).

The gas mains

Make sure everyone in the family knows how to turn off the gas supply at the mains. If you don't know where your gas tap is, it would be sensible to ask your meter reader the next time he calls. (It is usually a small lever on the gas pipe near your meter.)

OFF: Turn the lever until the notched line on the spindle points across the pipe. If your tap seems stiff, don't attempt to loosen it yourself – call your local gas service centre to come and loosen it for you safely, free of charge.
ON: Before turning the gas on again, make sure that all appliances and

pilot lights are turned off. The gas tap is on when the notched line on the spindle points along the pipe. After turning the supply back on, be sure to relight all pilot lights.

Tip When you go on holiday or leave your home empty for any length of time during the summer, turn the gas off.

Carbon monoxide poisoning

Have your gas- and oil-fired appliances regularly serviced, and don't forget that if any of your fuel-burning appliances (including gas central heating boilers, water-heaters, open fires and wood-burning stoves) uses a flue, it must be swept at least once a year to keep it clear. If the chimney or flue does get blocked, the waste gases could spill into the room, polluting the air you breathe with carbon monoxide. This could be fatal. Contact the National Association of Chimney Sweeps for details of chimney sweeps in your area – call free on 0800 833464.

Also make sure that all rooms containing gas fires are well-ventilated.

What to do if you smell gas

- Don't operate electrical switches – on or off. This includes light switches and door bells.
- Don't smoke or use matches or naked flames.
- Turn off the gas supply at the mains (next to the gas meter).
- Open doors and windows to get rid of the gas.
- Check to see if the gas has been left on or if a pilot light has been blown out If so, turn the appliance off.
- Phone the emergency gas service (look under Gas in the phone book, or better still, keep a list of emergency numbers handy).
- If you smell gas in the street outside, report it at once. Don't leave it to someone else to do.
- Don't forget to relight pilot lights once the gas supply has been safely turned back on.

Warning signs

If you notice any of the following signs on your gas appliances, stop using the appliance and contact your local gas office immediately.

- Is the outer case discoloured?
- Is the decoration around the appliance stained or discoloured?
- Does the appliance burn with a yellow or orange flame?
- Is there a strange smell when the appliance is on?
- Is the flue damaged or broken?

Domestic gas and carbon monoxide detectors

Gas Your sense of smell should tell you if there is a gas leak (which could lead to an explosion). But if you are worried about gas or have a poor sense of smell, consider having a gas detector installed (professionally, by wiring directly to the mains). There are different types of detector for natural and bottled gas, and each must be installed correctly: high on a wall to detect the lighter-than-air methane in natural gas, or low down for the heavier-than-air propane and butane in bottled gas.

Carbon monoxide This doesn't have a smell, so you will not be able to detect it unaided. A carbon monoxide detector will tell you if you have a leaky flue (which could lead to your getting poisoned).

You shouldn't rely on a gas or carbon monoxide detector to tell you if there is a leak. There is no substitute for making sure that all your gas appliances are properly maintained, have adequate ventilation and are serviced regularly.

If you are thinking about buying a gas or carbon monoxide detector, contact the Gas Consumers Council for advice. The telephone number of your local regional office can be found in the phone book or on the back of your gas bill. Alternatively, contact your local gas office (look under Gas in the phone book).

As yet there is no British Standard for gas or carbon monoxide detectors and neither organisation is able to recommend particular brands.

ELECTRICITY

House wiring

Faulty electrical wiring causes 2,200 fires and around ten deaths a year in Britain. You should have your household wiring checked every five years. This may sound excessive, but in reality the inspection cost is a small price to pay for electrical safety.

If your wiring circuits are more than 25 years old, or if your sockets are of the round two-pin type you almost certainly need to renew them. Before checking or repairing the wiring of sockets or switches, turn off the power at the mains.

Get expert help for all repairs and wiring. If you think there may be a fault, immediately contact a contractor who is approved by the National Inspection Council for Electrical Installation Contracting. There is a list of approved contractors at all Electricity Board showrooms. Do not attempt to repair it yourself.

Plugs, fuses and flexes

Faulty flexes cause 1,000 fires and several deaths a year in Britain. By following a few straightforward precautions on how to use electricity safely in your home, you can make sure your home is a safer place.

Electricity can be dangerous, so don't attempt complex repairs unless you have expert knowledge.

For safety, always buy plugs made to BS 1363, and look for reinforced

---

Emergency repair kit

It's worth assembling a small emergency kit to cope with simple electrical repairs. The kit should include:

- replacement fusewire or fuse for the mains fuse box (consumer unit)
- replacement 3 amp and 13 amp fuses for plugs
- a medium and a small screwdriver
- a roll of insulating tape
- a working torch in the event of a power cut.

shatter-proof plugs that meet BS 1363/A, if the appliance is constantly being plugged in and unplugged.

Don't overload plug sockets. Use adaptors as little as possible. Ideally, you should use a separate socket for every appliance but this is not always possible. If you regularly use two appliances from one point have it replaced with a double socket. It's worth it for the convenience, let alone the safety.

Make sure you are using the correct fuse for the appliance (*see* Which fuse? page 95).

Use short, undamaged flexes. The shorter, the safer – there's less to trip over or becomed damaged. Never staple a flex to the wall or skirting board, or run it under carpets or flooring.

Never handle plugs, switches or any electrical appliance with wet hands. Switch off and unplug appliances before cleaning and make sure they are thoroughly dry before use.

Check flexes and fittings regularly. Get into the habit of a quick check every time you use an appliance. Look out for wear, damage and loose connections particularly where the flex enters the plug. Also check for cracked or chipped plugs and sockets. Have any faults put right immediately.

When buying new electrical appliances, look for the BEAB Approved label (British Electrotechnical Approvals Board) or BSI Kitemark. It indicates that the appliance has been tested by an independent approval authority and it meets the appropriate safety standards.

Don't be tempted to buy electrical appliances second-hand, as they may not be safe.

Faulty appliances

If an appliance is not working properly, switch it off and pull the plug out before investigating.

Check that the plug is correctly wired and fused, making sure that the wires are held firmly in place at each terminal. Replace the fuse if necessary and check that the cable clamp in the plug firmly grips the outer plastic cover of the flex and not just the wires.

If a fuse in a plug or the mains fuse box (consumer unit) continues to blow, disconnect the appliance and have it checked by an expert.

If the protective covering of a flex becomes frayed, split or worn, replace it immediately. Use a single continuous length – never join two pieces of flex together.

If the wall socket becomes damaged or the wall shows signs of damp, consult a qualified electrician.

Step-by-step guide to wiring a plug

Wiring a plug is quite straightforward. You will need a small screwdriver and something to cut the wires and to strip away unwanted insulation – a proper wire stripper and cutter is best but you can use a sharp knife or scissors. If you are in any doubt whatsoever when wiring plugs or replacing fuses, stop what you're doing and get expert advice.

1 Unscrew the plug cover. Loosen one flex clamp/cord grip screw, and remove the other.
2 Remove the fuse. Carefully lever it out with a screwdriver if necessary. Loosen the terminal screws.
3 Position the flex in the plug, and cut the wires to reach about 13 mm (½ inch) beyond each terminal. It may be necessary to cut away the flex outer sheath.
4 Carefully strip enough insulation to expose about 6 mm/¼ in for screwhole terminals, or about 13 mm/½ in for clamp-type ones. Take care not to cut any strands of wire. Twist the strands of each wire together.

Remember the wire colour codes

- Blue wire to Neutral terminal (marked N)
- Brown wire to Live terminal (marked L)
- Green/Yellow wire to Earth terminal (marked E or ⏚)
  Some electrical appliances are double-insulated for extra protection. They are marked with a double square symbol. These appliances have only two wires and don't need to be earthed. All other equipment must be fitted with three-core cable including an earth wire.

5 Fasten the flex clamp/cord grip, checking that it firmly grips the outer sheath of the cable and not just the wires. Fit each wire into the appropriate terminal and tighten each screw. Check that there are no stray 'whiskers' of bare wire.

6 Fit the correct fuse (*see* Which fuse?, page 95), refit the plug cover and screw tight.

Easy wiring

If you find it difficult or are unsure how to wire a plug, look out for easy-to-wire plugs. They are generally much more expensive (nearly four times the price of a standard plug), but they are easier to wire. One example is the Rotaplug (around £3 from DIY stores) which doesn't even need a screwdriver. You simply cut the stripped wires to the same length before inserting them into the correct colour-coded channels. You then twist the plug pins to secure the wires and close the fuse cover.

Replacing a fuse in a plug

If a fuse blows, it's often a sign that there's something wrong with either the appliance or the plug or flex. Unless this is seen to, the fuse will blow again as soon as it is replaced.

1 If the appliance just doesn't work, try another socket before you think about replacing the fuse.

2 If you hear a bang when you switch on an appliance, the fuse has blown. Turn the appliance off at the mains and pull out the plug. (If you smell burning, or see black round the plug that could indicate charring, don't attempt to replace the fuse, but take the appliance for repair.)

3 Take the back off the plug and remove the old fuse. Check to see if any wires have come astray and make any necessary repairs before replacing the fuse.

Tip If you're not sure whether a fuse is working or not, try testing it on a metal torch. Unscrew the end and rest one end of the fuse on the casing and the other on the battery. If the fuse is working, the torch will light up.

Moulded plugs

From 1 February 1995, most domestic electrical appliances manufactured in or imported into the UK have had to be fitted with a correctly fused 13-amp plug. They are non-rewirable. To replace the fuse, switch off and unplug the appliance. Prise the fuse-holder out with a screwdriver, replace the fuse and refit the fuse-holder. Do not use a plug without a fuse-holder and never use a fuse greater than the size shown on the plug.

Should a moulded plug become damaged or faulty you should cut it off and make sure it is disposed of safely. Do not leave it where children may find it and plug it into a supply socket. Fit a new plug (*see* page 93).

Residual current devices

A residual current device (RCD) gives additional protection against electric shock if electrical equipment develops a fault or if you accidentally make contact with a live part. It can detect damage to the cable and other faults through change in the current flow. It then automatically cuts off the power to the equipment, reducing the risk of an accident and warning you that there is a fault.

Which fuse?

A cartridge fuse in an electrical plug protects you from an electric shock, so it's important to fit the correct fuse (conforming to BS 1362 approved by ASTA) for the appliance. The wattage of the appliance is usually marked on the rating plate. If a fuse blows, never fit a higher-rated fuse to get out of trouble.

3-amp fuse for most appliances up to 720 watts (w), including radios, table lamps, televisions (some TV manufacturers recommend a 5-amp fuse), electric blankets and stereos.

13-amp fuse for appliances over 720 watts (w), including irons, kettles, fan heaters, lawn-mowers, toasters, fridges and freezers, washing machines, vacuum cleaners and dishwashers.

RCDs can be fitted by a professional at the mains supply, to offer protection throughout the home. Alternatively, you can buy socket outlet RCDs which protect only the socket which is being used. These are suitable for portable equipment such as a lawn-mower or drill and appliances which need an extension lead. RCDs should be fitted to any electrical supply expected to serve appliances outdoors.

FIRE

No one should underrate the danger of fire. In this country every year there are around 55,000 accidental fires in the home which kill about 800 people and injure over 14,000 others.

Take some time now to think carefully about how you and your family would escape from your house in the event of a fire. Ask yourself the following questions:

- Is there an alternative route down in case the stairs are blocked by fire?
- Is there a window in every room that you could climb out of?
- If you have double glazing or window locks, is the key kept in a safe place for easy unlocking?

Take the following precautions so that you are fully prepared for the possibility of fire:

- Make sure you understand how to use fire extinguishers and fire blankets in the event of a fire.
- Make sure that everyone in the family knows what to do if there is a fire. Make an escape plan.
- Ensure the whereabouts of all keys to window locks and interior doors.

Tip Store family photographs, jewellery or important documents such as insurance policies, marriage and birth certificates in a fire-resistant storage container, such as the Sentry Fire-Safe Security Chest (around £30 from DIY stores).

Smoke alarms

Over 60 per cent of households now have a smoke alarm. Your chances of surviving a fire are two to three times greater if you have one fitted. Battery-operated models cost from as little as £4. You can also buy mains-powered alarms if you have a large house and

---

Smoke alarms for the hard-of-hearing

Smoke alarms are available for those with hearing impairment. For details contact the Royal National Institute for Deaf People.

---

need several alarms (prices from around £20). With these, you don't have to worry about battery replacement, but they must be fitted by a qualified electrician and should have battery back-up in case of power cuts. You should have at least one smoke alarm on each floor of the house – preferably interlinked so that if one goes off they all do, ensuring you hear the alarm.

There are two types of smoke alarm. Best for halls is a 'photo-electric' (optical) alarm that reacts quickly to slow, smouldering fires, such as those that start on upholstered furniture, but is less likely to react to smoke from burnt toast. On the upstairs landing, install an 'ionisation' alarm within earshot of the bedrooms – this responds quickly to fast, flaming fires.

A smoke alarm should comply with BS 5446, which indicates it is sufficiently sensitive to smoke, and should preferably carry the BSI Kitemark. A mains-operated smoke alarm must comply with current Institution of Electrical Engineers (IEE) Wiring Regulations. Always use a qualified electrician for installation.

Position Site the smoke alarm in a position that allows routine maintenance, testing and cleaning and is well away from areas where steam, condensation or fumes could give false alarms, and from areas that get very hot or cold.

Position it within 7 m/23 ft of rooms where fires are likely to start and within 3 m/10 ft of bedroom doors; at least 30 cm/12 in from any wall, or from a light fitting fixed to the ceiling; or, if wall mounted, between 15 cm/6 in and 30 cm/12 in below the ceiling.

What to do in the event of a fire

- Get everyone out quickly by the safest route. If you have to go through a smoked-filled area, crawl and keep your head low.
- Call the fire brigade as soon as possible from a neighbour's house. Don't go back inside your house to use the phone.
- If it's safe, shut doors to delay the spread of fire and smoke.
- Only attempt to tackle a fire in its early stages. Don't risk injury to fight a fire.
- Don't go back to the house until the fire brigade tells you it is safe.

Maintenance Once you have fitted a smoke alarm, it is easy to forget about it. But it is important to maintain it properly – it could save your life.

- Make a note in your diary to replace the battery once a year (whether it needs it or not).
- Most have a test button which sets off the alarm when pressed – test the battery once a week.
- Vacuum dust from inside the alarm.
- Test the sensor annually by waving a smoking candle under it.

Fire-fighting equipment

For most homes, a fire blanket (conforming to BS 6575) in the kitchen and a multi-purpose dry powder, foam or water-type extinguisher (conforming to BS 5423 or BS 6165 and the BSI Kitemark) in the hall would be adequate. But it depends on the fire risks in your home and what you can afford. A multi-purpose dry powder or foam extinguisher in the garage, shed or car would complete the package.

If in doubt about which type to have, contact your local fire brigade for advice or contact the Fire Protection Association for useful leaflets.

Chapter 13

DIY and Garden Safety

One of the biggest causes of home accidents is the enthusiastic amateur who overlooks the essential precautions when using power tools, hazardous chemicals or even ladders.

DIY SAFETY

It is essential not to tackle jobs beyond your capability and to be aware of the risks which go with virtually all DIY jobs, particularly where power tools are involved. If you are at all unsure, call in the professionals.

- Never cut corners. Use the right tool for the job and keep tools in good working order. Always follow the manufacturer's safety instructions.
- When drilling walls, avoid areas adjacent to power sockets and the area at right angles and vertically above them. Power cables are usually routed in these locations.
- If the job is dangerous or harmful, always wear the appropriate protective clothing, such as gloves, face masks, safety goggles, ear defenders and knee pads.
- Prepare yourself and your working area properly before you begin.
- Fuels, glue, cleaners, paints and lubricants all contain chemicals that can be harmful. Always follow the maker's safety guidelines. Ensure that you have adequate ventilation.
- Use a residual current device (RCD) when operating power tools (*see* Electricity, page 91).
- Put blade covers on knives and chisels when not using them.
- Keep children away from all DIY work.

Ladder safety

Falling off ladders and chairs is one of the most frequent DIY accidents. Ladders should be placed on firm, level ground 1m/3 ft away from the wall for every 4 m/13 ft of height. The top of the ladder should overlap the highest point and if possible be tied in place. Secure the base with a sandbag, or tie the ladder to wooden pegs knocked into the ground. If the ground is soggy, place the ladder on a board to make it secure.

- Always check that a ladder is suitable for the job.
- Use a special ladder tray that fits on to the ladder instead of carrying paint or tools. This allows you to have both hands free for better balance and safety.
- Ensure that a stepladder is extended fully and the top step is locked firmly in position before using.
- Never over-extend an extension ladder or exceed the recommended angle of a ladder.
- Always make sure that the feet of the ladder are on a firm and level surface and the top is resting on something solid, not a drainpipe or guttering. Use stabilising legs when using a ladder extension.
- Always wear a tool belt (which can hold a number of tools) rather than carrying a handful.

GARDEN SAFETY

Each year an estimated 300,000 people need hospital treatment for injuries caused by accidents in the garden. The most obvious danger is the use of electrical equipment such as mowers and hedge trimmers. However, other potential hazards ranging from the use and storing of pesticides to barbecues must also be considered. Even the plants in the garden may be a hazard.

In a garden where children play, it is important to cover ponds and pools with substantial netting which will prevent them from falling in. Even shallow water should be covered since it's possible for a small child to drown in a depth of water as little as 7.5 cm/3 in.

Do not use electrical appliances outside when it's raining. Never use any garden equipment barefoot or with open sandals. Wear trousers and strong flat-heeled, rubber-soled shoes.

Check all plugs, wiring and equipment for damage and worn or loose parts before you start. Don't repair damaged cables – get them replaced. When buying new electrical gardening tools, look for the BEAB safety approval and BSI Kitemark.

Always switch off and unplug electrical equipment before making any adjustments or cleaning it and put away after use. Have it serviced every two or three years by a qualified electrician.

Each year check terraces, steps and paths for uneven paving or cracks which could prove hazardous. Clean concrete paths and patios to remove any grime and algae which can become slimy when it gets wet. A pressure washer is a fast and effective way of doing this. Alternatively, sweep with a stiff broom, then treat with a 1:8 solution of bleach and water. Scrub then repeat the treatment. Leave to dry before brushing the area clean. For stubborn stains, use a proprietary path cleaner.

Lawn-mowers
- Before mowing the lawn, remove loose stones or debris.
- Keep the flex behind you away from moving blades to avoid cutting it. Either trail it over your shoulder or hold a short loop in one hand.
- Cut away from and not towards the flex. Be especially careful with hover-type mowers which can easily drift back over your foot or the flex. Always wear shoes when mowing.
- Always switch off and unplug before clearing grass from a mower.

Hedgetrimmers and chainsaws
- Keep the flex away from moving blades and ensure it stays behind you.
- Always keep both hands on the handle.
- Wear protective clothing including strong gloves and safety goggles.
- Make sure the timber being cut is securely positioned.

Outdoor wiring and extension leads
- Use a single flex without joins and never work with wet or worn ones.

- If you don't have easy access to a socket outlet indoors, get a qualified electrician to install a special waterproof socket and protect it with a residual current device (*see* Electricity, page 91).
- When using an extension lead, make sure that it is fully unwound (it could overheat if rolled up) and of sufficient current capacity. It must have rubber connections if used outdoors.

Pesticides and fungicides

A wide variety of garden chemicals, including pesticides, weed-killers, fungicides and fertilisers, are available to the gardener today. Some garden

---

Plant safety labelling

The Horticultural Trades Association has drawn up a voluntary code of practice for the labelling of poisonous and potentially harmful plants, bulbs and seeds. The Code sets out guidelines for the retailing of plants to ensure that the consumer is informed of potentially harmful plants at the point of purchase.

The Code identifies 64 plants or plant groups as being potentially harmful. These plants have been categorised into three groups according to the degree of harm they can cause, along with suggested labelling recommendations:

A Most harmful; poisonous if eaten. Skin contact commonly causes severe blistering dermatitis. Includes only one plant group: Rhus radicans, succedanea, verniciflua. The code suggests that the sale of these plants to the public should be restricted and discouraged.

B Toxic if eaten, may cause skin allergy; skin and eye irritant. Plants listed include aconitum, laburnum and digitalis (foxglove).

C Harmful if eaten; may cause skin allergy; and skin and eye irritant. Plants listed include helleborus, iris and wisteria.

The introduction of these voluntary recommendations will be gradual. You should see loose bulbs with warning signs in place by September 1995 and on plants by September 1997.

---

chemicals are potentially dangerous and should be treated with caution. If the instructions are followed precisely, chemicals should prove effective with little risk to the user or to the environment. Always take the following precautions:

- Choose the chemical carefully — make sure it is the right one for the job. Follow the manufacturer's instructions and any warning messages carefully. Apply at the rate and frequency stated on the label. Never mix chemicals unless the manufacturer recommends this.
- Avoid contact with the skin and eyes and don't inhale dust, smoke or sprays. Never eat, drink or smoke when applying a chemical.
- Dispose of any excess carefully and wash out any spray equipment thoroughly. Don't use spray equipment for anything other than chemicals.
- Keep pets and children away during treatment. Store chemicals out of reach of children and animals and keep them in their original containers, with their original labels and any explanatory leaflets.

Plants

Think carefully before siting hazardous plants where they will be accessible and attractive to children or animals. If in doubt about a plant take a clipping to your local garden centre (wear protective gardening gloves). Children find it hard to tell the difference between berries and fruits that are safe to eat – like blackberries – and berries that can hurt them so teach them not to eat anything in the garden, just in case.

The most common plants with poisonous leaves, seeds or berries are laburnum, yew, foxgloves, deadly nightshade, privet, laurel, rhododendron and hydrangea.

Although cases of fatal poisoning are rare, never ignore plant warnings and if your child has eaten parts of, or been poisoned by, an unknown plant, seek medical advice immediately. Don't make him or her sick, and take a sample of the plant with you.

Outdoor glazing

Consider installing safety glazing (toughened or laminated glass or plastic sheet glazing) in the conservatory, patio doors, at low levels, and any balustrades. Contact the Glass and Glazing Federation for further advice and local member stockists.

Barbecues and bonfires

- Light bonfires and site barbecues a good distance from the house away from trees and fences.
- Keep children away.
- Never use petrol or other flammable fluids to start bonfires or barbecues.
- Read the instructions and follow the procedure for how to start or relight a barbecue safely. The quality of charcoal varies from brand to brand. The better the quality the easier the barbecue will be to light and keep lit. (The British Standard for barbecues is BS 5258.)

Chapter 14

First Aid

You never know when accidents will happen. Having some basic knowledge of first aid can prove invaluable – there is nothing worse than the feeling of despair if you can't help. Many minor accidents can be effectively treated at home. Anyone can learn the basics of first aid and invest in a practical kit. Proper training is essential if you are to tackle serious emergencies but the following guidelines should enable you to cope with minor injuries.

ACTION IN EMERGENCIES

If you are faced with an accident or emergency in your home or garden, do the following:

- Keep calm and reassure the casualty.
- Assess the situation – is there any danger to you or your casualty?
- Remember hygiene – always wash your hands before and after handling wounds.
- Don't give the person anything to eat or drink. Don't let them smoke.
- If serious, or there is doubt, call an ambulance.

First-aid kit

- sterile dressings of different sizes
- triangular and crêpe bandages
- cotton wool
- individually wrapped assorted plasters
- sterile gauze pads
- safety pins
- scissors
- tweezers
- thermometer
- mild painkillers
- antiseptic liquid or cream (keep an eye on the 'use-by' dates)

Shock

Shock can arise as a result of injury or stress. The severity of shock depends upon the nature and extent of the injury and may vary from a feeling of faintness, or nausea, to sudden death in the most severe cases. It is important to take the following measures:

- Constantly reassure the casualty.
- Treat any obvious injuries such as severe bleeding, but don't move the casualty unnecessarily. Lay the casualty down and raise and support their legs if possible.
- Keep the casualty warm by wrapping a blanket or coat around them. Do not give them anything to eat, drink or smoke.
- Seek medical attention.

Bleeding

- Control severe bleeding by covering the wound with a sterile dressing and applying direct pressure.
- If a wound is gaping or if there are any foreign bodies such as glass embedded in the wound, press the edges together. Don't attempt to remove the embedded object.
- Lay the casualty down and, if possible, raise and support the injured part.
- Apply a dressing and bandage firmly. If blood seeps through, apply another dressing over the top.
- For minor wounds and grazes, lightly rinse under running water. Pat dry with a clean tissue and apply a plaster.

Burns and scalds

- Immerse the injured part in cold running water for at least ten minutes, preferably longer, until the pain subsides.
- Quickly remove rings, bangles or watches before any swelling develops.
- Cover with a loose dressing - don't use adhesive plasters.
- To avoid infection don't burst blisters.
- Don't use any ointment or creams on the burn.

- Don't remove clothing sticking to the burn.
- Burns larger than the size of your hand should be seen by a doctor.

Choking

Remember that this can be life-threatening.

- Remove any debris or false teeth from the casualty's mouth and encourage coughing.
- Give the casualty up to five sharp slaps on the back between the shoulder blades. For a baby or infant, hold them head down on your lap, supporting the upper body with one hand and give much lighter slaps to the back.
- If slaps don't work use the abdominal thrust. With an adult, stand or kneel behind them. Put your arms around their waist and clasp your hands together in front above their navel. Now give a sharp pull upwards and inwards. Repeat up to four times. Carefully remove the obstruction from the mouth. (*Do not* give abdominal thrusts to a young child or baby.)

Nose bleeds

- Sit the casualty down with head slightly forward.
- Instruct them to breathe through their mouth and pinch the soft part of the nose firmly for about ten minutes. Release and reapply if necessary.
- Warn the casualty not to blow their nose for several hours.
- If the bleeding does not stop within half an hour, the casualty should receive medical attention.

Wasp and bee stings

- If the sting is left embedded in the skin, carefully remove it with tweezers. Don't squeeze the skin, or this will spread the venom.
- Apply a cold compress of ice to relieve pain and reduce swelling (even a bag of frozen peas covered in a towel will do).
- **Warning** Some people can develop a major allergic reaction to bee and wasp stings within minutes and need medical attention.

Tetanus

Gardeners are at particular risk from tetanus. After immunisation, they should have booster jabs every ten years. A gardener with a wound should attend hospital or visit a doctor for a booster if their injections are out-of-date. Ensure that all the family have had tetanus inoculations in case any garden accident should occur.

FIRST-AID COURSES

The best way to learn resuscitation and other first aid is from a trained instructor. St John Ambulance and the British Red Cross offer first-aid courses. They also have a variety of leaflets on safety and first aid. The telephone directory will give details of your local branch.

FURTHER HELP

For further information on safety in the home in general, contact the Royal Society for the Prevention of Accidents (RoSPA) (*see* Useful Addresses).

Chapter 15

Car Safety

In 1993, the most recent year for which Department of Transport figures are available, around 3,800 people were killed and a further 45,000 were seriously injured in road accidents in Britain.

The number of people killed or injured in road accidents has reduced over the last decade. In 1993 the figures were the lowest since records began in 1926. Safety experts partially attribute the falling numbers to better-designed and built cars. Certainly a great part of the injury reduction is due to the wearing of seat-belts.

SAFETY FEATURES

Car safety has become a major consideration when buying a new car, particularly for the family. Public awareness has provoked car manufacturers into intense competition with safety features and many are now fitting airbags, side impact bars, and anti-lock braking as standard (or offering them as an option).

Airbags

The airbag is a nylon cushion which rapidly inflates with nitrogen when sensors in the car detect the onset of a severe impact in the event of a collision. The bags inflate and begin to deflate instantly, cushioning the impact. Inflation takes just $1/20$th of a second, faster than the blink of an eye.

An airbag's function is to prevent your head and torso striking hard parts of the car interior, such as the steering wheel, which could cause injury. Even when you are wearing a seat-belt this can happen; an airbag provides additional protection, although, normally, only in frontal collisions.

Front-seat passengers generally have less to gain than drivers but passenger-side airbags are increasingly being offered either as standard or as an optional extra.

Young children must *never* be carried in a rear-facing infant carrier on the front passenger seat of any car fitted with a passenger-side airbag – the inflating airbag can deliver a dangerous blow. Strap the infant carrier in the back seat of the car instead.

Anti-lock brakes

If you lock the wheels of a car during emergency braking, you lose steering control and are likely to spin or to skid into whatever is ahead. An anti-lock braking system (ABS) prevents this loss of control by applying and releasing the brakes automatically to ensure the wheels never lock, however hard you press the brake pedal and however slippery the road.

ABS brakes are of great benefit in emergencies, but should not be provoked into operation during normal driving. They will not improve your car's braking performance on gravel or snow, nor will they reduce braking distances on dry surfaces. They should not be relied on to do so on any road surface. You must not try to 'pump' ABS brakes yourself because pumping prevents effective operation.

Head restraints

One safety feature that nearly all cars are fitted with is a head restraint. Yet because many are used incorrectly they offer little benefit in an accident. Many people still refer to the padded bit at the top of the driver's seat as a head rest. It isn't. It is a head restraint and, used properly, can prevent or reduce whiplash or more serious injuries which are so common in road accidents particularly as a result of rear impacts.

To be effective, they must be correctly positioned, with the top of the restraint roughly at eye level. Ideally, it should be in contact with the back of your head when you're sitting in a comfortable driving position. A poorly adjusted head restraint could act as a pivot to the neck, with terrible results.

If your car seats lack head restraints, ask your dealer whether they can be fitted. Often it is a simple operation.

Side impact bars

Side impacts, though less common than frontal ones, account for a quarter of all deaths and serious injuries among car occupants.

Whereas in a head-on crash there is plenty of bodywork and hardware to progressively absorb the energy of the impact, in a side impact there is precious little.

Side impact bars – aluminium beams or bars in the car's doors – are intended to limit intrusion into the passenger space and thereby prevent or lessen injury.

Controversy currently surrounds their effectiveness. The simple additon of a side impact bar to strengthen the car door will not necessarily improve your chances of escaping serious injury. Some safety experts actually claim that side impact bars could in fact increase the severity of injuries and even act as a locking bolt in a frontal impact, making it harder for the rescue services to force the door open.

However, side impact protection has been included by most car manufacturers. Volvo, which pioneered side impact bars, claim that their research suggests that side impact bars reduce the incident of personal injury by about 25 per cent. Unfortunately, until conclusive results are produced, you, as the consumer, are left to make your own judgement.

Seat-belts

It is estimated that over 4,000 lives have been saved and 77,000 serious injuries avoided since wearing seat-belts was made compulsory.

The law does not prevent you from carrying more passengers than there are belts, but belts should be used if they are available. It is illegal to carry an unrestrained child in the front seat of any vehicle.

Pregnant women Even if you are pregnant you are required by law to wear a seat-belt in both the front and rear seats where belts are fitted. It may become awkward or uncomfortable but it is still safer to wear one. The following is the best way for anyone to wear a seat-belt – pregnant or not.

• Put the lap part of the belt across your hips, making sure the belt goes under, not across the baby.

Seat-belts and the law			
	Front seat	**Rear seat**	**Whose responsibility**
Driver	Seat-belt must be worn if fitted		Driver
Child under 3 years of age	Appropriate child restraint must be used	Appropriate child restraint must be used if available	Driver
Child aged 3 to 11 and under 1.5 m/ approx. 5ft in height	Appropriate child restraint must be worn if available. If not, an adult seat-belt must be worn	Appropriate child restraint must be worn if available. If not, an adult seat-belt must be worn if available	Driver
Child aged 12 or 13, or younger child 1.5 m/ approx 5ft or more in height	Adult seat-belt must be worn if available	Adult seat-belt must be worn if available	Driver
Adult passengers	Seat-belt must be worn if available	Seat-belt must be worn if available	Passenger

- Put the diagonal strap around the baby and across your chest.
- If you are driving a car with an airbag, move the seat back as far as is practical. If you are a passenger in a car with a front passenger airbag, push your seat back as far as possible or travel in the back using a three-point belt.
- Never try to pad the seat-belt to make it more comfortable. Either the padding could slip out or it could concentrate the force of impact over your abdomen in a crash.
- Always wear seat-belts as tight as possible. Any slack can drastically increase the force and risk of injury in an accident.

- Check your seat position especially in the later stages of pregnancy and readjust after the birth.

CAR MAINTENANCE

Very few people, men or women, lift the bonnet on their car but almost 50 per cent of breakdowns attended by breakdown organisations such as the RAC and AA are caused by lack of car maintenance. With regular vehicle checks and servicing, your car is less likely to break down and is safer to drive.

Regular checks

- Check the oil level on the dipstick about once a month, a little more often if the car is new or your mileage is high. It should be between the maximum and minimum marks. If you have to top up your oil, add small amounts at a time and use a funnel.
- Check the water in the header tank (or radiator on older models). Remember – never do this when the engine is hot.
- Prior to winter, top up to the correct level on the header tank with a mixture of water and anti-freeze in the right ratio. Check the vehicle's handbook.
- Check that the battery terminals are tight. Clean and smear them with petroleum jelly (not normal grease). Unless you have a 'sealed for life' battery, check every three months that the fluid covers the plates, and top up with distilled water if necessary.
- Check the fan belt. If it's frayed or very slack, get a garage to change it.
- Fill the screen washer bottle using an additive in the water to stop smearing and in winter use a special windscreen washer fluid.
- Spray all ignition electrics with an anti-damp aerosol.
- Check all tyre pressures – including the spare – according to the car's handbook using an accurate gauge. Even a correctly inflated tyre only has about the same contact with the road at speed as an A5 sheet of paper.
- Check your tyre tread and ensure that there are no bald patches. There should be a minimum of 1.6 mm tread on all parts of the tyre.

Tip As a quick guide to tyre tread, place a 5p piece in the tread. If the number five is partially or completely obscured the tread is good and the tyre is safe. If, however, the number five shows, the tyre is illegal and very dangerous. Change it immediately.

- Check all lights both front and rear, replacing bulbs as and when needed. If you have no one to help you check them, park up against a wall and look at the reflections.

GOING ON HOLIDAY

If you're planning a long car journey or motoring holiday, ensure your car has a thorough service two weeks beforehand. If a service is not due, carry out the following spot checks to prepare the car for safe motoring.

- Check oil level.
- Top up screen washer bottle.
- Check water level in header tank (radiator).
- Check tyre pressure, including the spare.
- Clean lights, front and rear.
- Clean windscreen inside and out. Finish with a rag soaked in methylated spirits to prevent smears.
- If towing a caravan, check the caravan tyres for wear and make sure you take a spare.
- Don't overload your car. Pack heavy luggage first and make sure it is firmly secured. Adjust your tyre pressure to cope with the additional weight of luggage in accordance with your manufacturer's manual.
- Make sure roof racks are securely fixed and luggage is firmly strapped on.

CHILD CAR SEATS

Every year about 80 children are killed and more than 12,000 are injured whilst travelling in cars. Three-quarters of these lives could be saved and two-thirds of the injuries avoided if children were properly restrained every time they travelled by car. In 1989, it became law for children under

14 to be restrained in rear seats of cars where appropriate restraints are fitted, and it's estimated that rear seat-belts currently save 140 lives and prevent 1,800 serious injuries each year.

In an accident, an unrestrained child can be thrown forward against the dashboard or even through a window with a force equivalent to the weight of a baby elephant, even at low speeds.

Even for short journeys children should be correctly restrained. It is not safe to hold a baby or small child in your arms or in a sling. In a crash, you could not hold on to your baby, or the child might be crushed between you and the dashboard or car seat.

A seat-belt encircling both you and the child could also result in the child being crushed and receiving serious injuries.

The safest way for a child to travel in a car is by using a child restraint system that suits the child's weight and size, is properly used and is correctly fitted.

Child restraints should be selected on the basis of weight rather than the child's age. Recommended ages given by child-seat manufacturers are approximate and should only be used as a guideline. There are three stages of child seat, each designed to provide the best protection as your child grows. Some seats are designed to last for more than one stage.

Stage one: Baby
0–10 kg/22 lb (birth to 9 months approx).

Portable rear-facing infant carrier   The safest type of restraint for babies is an approved rear-facing infant carrier. Look for a seat that conforms to ECE R44.02 and/or BS AU202(a). (ECE is a regulation issued by the Economic Commission for Europe.) The seat can usually be fitted in the front or rear seat of the car and is held in place by a three-point lap and diagonal seat-belt. Fitting in the front seat is most popular because it allows mum or dad to drive whilst at the same time keeping a watchful eye on baby. It has its own harness which keeps the baby secure in the seat.

Babies have bigger heads and smaller bodies than adults so their centre of gravity is a lot higher. They also have weak necks that cannot support their head. Because of this, a child seat in the rear-facing position, incorporating an energy-absorption pad, is considered best for young babies because it avoids too much pressure being put on the baby's spine.

Remember You *must not* use a rear-facing infant carrier in the front seat of a car fitted with a passenger-side airbag. In these circumstances, use it only on the back seat.

Two-way seat These seats cover the needs of both babies and young children – stage one and stage two. Look for a seat that conforms to BS AU202(a) and BS 3254: Part 2 1988 and/or ECE R44.02. This type of seat is designed to be used as a rear-facing carrier for an infant up to 10 kg/ 22 lb (or for the first 6 to 9 months) and then turned round and used as a forward-facing child seat, from 10 kg/22 lb (once the child is able to hold its head up), until the child reaches 18 kg/40 lb (around 4 years). In both modes, the seat is usually held in position by an adult three-point seat-belt. In forward-facing mode, some seats can also be fitted with a lap belt. Although a two-way seat is cheaper than buying two separate seats, it can be larger and heavier than a standard infant carrier. This can make them more difficult to install or remove and they are not portable.

Carrycot with restraining straps This provides much less protection than a rear-facing infant carrier. It only secures the carrycot by means of a harness bolted to the car body, but not fastened to the baby. In an accident the baby could still be flung out of the carrycot and through a window. The carrycot is not designed to withstand the forces involved in an accident and, because of its shape and size, can only be used in the rear seat. They are not tested or approved as a restraint system for vehicles and are therefore not suitable for carrying children in the car.

Stage two: Young Child
9–18 kg/20–40 lb (6–9 months to 4 years approx).

Forward-facing child seat with integral harness Once a child is able to sit up unaided and hold its head up, it can travel in a forward-facing child seat. Look for a seat that conforms to BS 3254: Part 2 1988 and/or

ECE R44.02. The child is carried in a sitting position and restrained by a harness. Ensure the harness is adjustable and holds the child firmly. There are a number of options available offering a variety of features. Some seats can be reclined slightly to enable the child to sleep more comfortably on long car journeys.

If rear seat-belts are already fitted to your car, then a child seat which can be secured by existing seat-belts offers good flexibility, especially if you have two cars. Some forward-facing child seats can be held in place by a lap-belt, which is now fitted in most cars in the centre of the rear seat. This leaves other seat-belts free for booster or booster seats.

If there are no rear seat-belts or if a child seat can't be tightly fitted using the adult seat-belt, then choose a car seat that can be secured with a fitting kit. These simply fit to the lower seat-belt anchorage points on the car to allow the car seat to be securely fastened. Even if you don't have rear seat-belts, your car may still have anchorage points since these have been compulsory in all new cars since 1981. If not, anchorage points can be drilled if necessary. Ensure that you use the correct-fitting kit for your make and model of car seat.

Booster seat/Combination seat Another alternative for young children is a booster seat. The weight range varies from seat to seat but they are usually suitable for children weighing from 9 kg/20 lb to 25 kg/55 lb (aged between 6–9 months and 6 years).These are designed to improve the positioning of a three-point adult seat-belt for a small child. The seat-belt secures the seat into the car and the child into the seat, usually with the help of a locking device to guide the seat-belt correctly.

Warning For younger children – aged between 9 months and 3 years, booster seats must be used with a static seat-belt as opposed to the more modern inertia belt. If your car doesn't have static seat-belts, you must use a special fitting kit.

Booster seats are very convenient to use. They're lightweight and easy to fit, move from car to car and they require no special installation kit. Look for a booster seat that conforms to ECE R44.02. But remember, a child seat with its own harness will provide more support and protection for a young child than a booster seat.

Combination seats can be converted into a booster allowing a child to use the seat for longer. As your child grows, the seat back can be removed to become a booster, extending the seat's upper weight limit to 36 kg/ 80 lb (at around 11 years). Make sure it conforms to BS AU185 and/or ECE R44.02.

Stage three: Older child
18–36 kg/40–80 lb (3–4 years to 11 years approx).

Booster This is designed to raise a small child up to a level where an adult three-point seat-belt can be safely positioned across the child's shoulder and pelvis and not dangerously across the neck and stomach. Never use a booster with a lap-belt. The extra height provided by a booster allows a child to see out of the window, helping to avoid travel sickness. Look for a booster that conforms to BS AU185 and/or ECE R44.02.

A booster is held securely in place by the seat-belt and is specially shaped to guide the lap part of the seat-belt over the child's lap and hold the booster in place in the event of a crash. For this reason don't be tempted to use a seat-belt with a normal household cushion. The child could slip under the belt and be severely injured in an accident.

Some boosters are fitted with a strap which connects to the shoulder section of the adult belt. This allows you to adjust the seat-belt and ensure that it is correctly positioned over the child's shoulder. You can also buy separate seat-belt adjusters.

Safety aspects
- Not all car seats fit all cars. Different-shaped seats, upholstery, seat-belt webbing lengths and the position of seat-belt anchorage points can all affect child-seat fitment. Always try the child seat in your car first before buying.
- The safest position to fit a child seat is in the centre of the rear seat as this is likely to be furthest away from any structures in the event of a

crash. It also leaves the two three-point belts free for other passengers. Not all child seats can be properly or safely fitted here and a fitting kit may be required. However, having a child belted up anywhere in the car – including the front seat – is safer than travelling unrestrained, and less likely to distract the driver.

- Always read and follow the manufacturer's fitting instructions carefully. It is essential that all child seats be fitted correctly. Recent surveys by the RAC revealed that many were wrongly fitted, making them virtually useless.

- Fit child seats as tightly as possible into the car so they cannot be excessively moved forward or sideways. Push the child seat firmly into the seat upholstery and pull seat-belt webbing as tight as possible.

- Secure children tightly into the child-seat harness on every journey. Remember any slack can dramatically increase the force on a child in an accident.

- Never modify child seats or seat-belts in any way.

- Never tie, turn or cover buckles to prevent children playing with them as this could seriously hamper quick release from the car in an accident.

- Any child seat involved in an accident should be replaced even if it looks undamaged. Never buy a second-hand car seat – you don't know if it has been involved in an accident.

The In-Car Safety Centre stocks a range of child seats and safety accessories. They can also offer advice.

LAP-BELTS

Lap-belts are not the best way to restrain children of any age and are not as effective as an adult three-point seat-belt.

The problem is that the middle rear seat-belt in the majority of cars in Britain only straps over the lap. And since the law was changed to say that all occupants must wear seat-belts where fitted, several children and teenagers have been horribly injured by these belts in accidents.

Lap-belts are designed to fit around the hips of an adult, stopping them from being flung forward in a collision. But on children and teenagers, they sometimes sit across the abdomen, and can almost slice them in two in an accident. In the event of a collision at 45 km/30 miles per hour, a child of 8 to 12 has the equivalent weight of a baby elephant and is thrown into the strap with immense force. This causes the head, torso and legs to be thrown forwards violently, putting massive strain on the spine and internal organs. A child wearing a traditional three-point seat-belt stands a far smaller risk of injury, as the belt retains the upper body.

Safety for children

- Over-3s are safest using a booster and three-point belt. (Some child seats can take a child up to 6 or 11 years.)
- A lap-belt is better than nothing. It should be tight.
- Restrict the use of lap-belts to adults and older children whenever possible. If it's unavoidable to have a child in a lap-belt, put an under-3-year-old in a child seat, secured with a fitting kit in the lap-belt position. While for older children 15–25 kg/33–55 lb or 3½–7 years or who are too big for a child seat, a safer option is the Römer Vario restraint, priced around £35. This cushioned 'table' prevents the belt coming into direct contact with the child's body and stops the body jackknifing in the event of a crash. For stockist details, contact Britax.
- If using a child seat, position it in the middle rear seat, if possible, leaving the three-point belts free for other children.
- Don't use a booster with lap-belts. It is liable to slip out in an emergency stop.
- Be sure the lap-belt sits below the bony points of the pelvis.
- It's safer for a child to sit in front with a three-point belt than in the back with a lap-belt. It is not illegal for a child to be in front – the law states that a child under 3 years must use an appropriate child restraint for their weight, size and age. Over-3s must wear an adult seat-belt, if the appropriate child restraint is not available.
- If your car has only lap-belts in the back, you can in many cars have the outer seats converted to three-point. Most middle lap-belts cannot be converted safely.

Chapter 16

Bicycle Safety

Cycling is fun and a good way of keeping fit and is becoming increasingly popular. Around 20 million people in Britain now own a bicycle. But every year around 24,000 cyclists are killed or injured on our roads, about a third of whom are children. To enjoy your bike safely, you need to look after it well, and take particular care whenever you're out on the roads.

BUYING A BIKE

Look for a bike that conforms to the British Standard for safety - BS 6102. However, this is a manufacturing standard and is only fully effective if the bicycle is correctly assembled. When you buy a bike 'flat-packed' in a box such as those from a mail order company, *you* then become responsible for ensuring that it is assembled correctly and to the BS standard.

The best place to buy a bike is a specialist bicycle retailer who has a full range of styles and sizes available. The bikes are fully assembled and safety-checked so you can rest assured that it is safe to ride. Visit two or three specialists and discuss your requirements. Remember, price should not be your only consideration. Some cycle dealers may even allow you to have a test ride before you buy, to make sure the bike is right for you. (Don't be surprised if you're asked for a deposit, or some other form of security, before you are allowed to take the bike out of the shop.)

Most good dealers will be members of the Association of Cycle Traders. Look for the ACT sign in the shop window, or contact the ACT for details of your nearest specialist dealer.

Choosing the right type

A wide variety of models are available, so think about the type of riding you might do before you buy.

The most popular bikes today are mountain bikes (MTB). These are tough bikes designed for riding cross-country although some models are designed for the leisure cyclist and the commuter, while the more expensive versions are for off-road racing. Typical features are straight handlebars, thick tyres with knobbly tread for good shock absorbence and manoeuvrability, and a good range of gears. The more robust they are, the more you'll pay. You can even find mountain bike styling on bikes for 3 – 5-year-olds, but not all children's mountain bikes are designed for off-road use – some are merely imitations.

The latest type available is the hybrid bike. These have mountain bike styling, but are lighter and more responsive, with larger wheels and thinner tyres. They are less tough than mountain bikes and are more suitable for normal commuting.

For short commuting journeys around town, a traditional roadster or shopper will be adequate. These are designed for street use only. Special folding bikes are also available that collapse small enough to put in the boot of the car, making storage easier.

For the more serious cyclist, sporting, touring and racing bikes are available. Your specialist cycle dealer will be able to give further advice on your choice.

Get the right fit

The right size of bike is essential. A proper riding position can make the world of difference to the enjoyment and safety of cycling.

- Bikes are sized according to wheel diameter and frame height. The inside leg measurement determines the frame size you need. Bike sizes refer to the distance from the top of the seat tube to the bottom bracket axle (the point at which the pedals join the bike).
- To buy the right size of bike, measure your inside leg – the distance from crotch to floor, standing bare-foot – and deduct 23 cm/9 in. (The result will be roughly two-thirds your inside-leg measurement.) There are other formulae you can use but none is a substitute for actually sitting on the bike and trying it out for size.
- Make sure the bike is the correct length. You should not have to

stretch forward to reach the handlebars. If the frame length is correct, you should be able to touch the middle of the handlebars with your fingertips while your elbow rests just in front of the saddle.

- Check the distance between brakes and handlebars and make sure the brakes are not too stiff to use. This is especially important for children, whose hands are smaller and can't grip as well as an adult.
- Don't be tempted to buy a bigger size for a child to grow into. Too big a bike will be heavy, uncomfortable, difficult to steer, and dangerous. It may even put them off riding.
- Once you've got the right bike size, you can adjust the saddle and handlebars to give the best position for cycling. When adjusting the saddle, your bare heel should rest on the pedal, at its lowest point, with your leg straight (neither stretched or bent). Another important check is when sitting on the saddle, you should be able to rest the ball of your foot on the floor. For beginners, the saddle should be positioned lower until they feel more secure.
- Handlebars should be adjusted to roughly the same level as the saddle.
- When adjusting the saddle and handlebars, leave at least 5 cm/2 in of the tube inside the frame. (Most are marked to show the minimum depth that must be left inside the frame.)
- Some children find it hard to learn to balance on a bike and need stabilisers. But only use bike stabilisers if your child has real problems. They help a learner get over the initial fear of the bike, but it only puts off the day when balance must be learned. Take them off before he or she comes to depend on them.

CYCLE TRAINING

Cycling awareness and an understanding of cycle safety are very important at any age. Before you start cycling, you must be certain that you have basic riding skills.

If you're not used to riding, or are teaching children to ride, practise in a safe place first, away from roads, and gradually move on to quiet roads as your confidence grows. Don't forget that, as a cyclist on a road, you must obey the traffic laws at all times – so make sure you know your Highway Code.

It's a good idea for children to attend a cycle training course. The most common is the National Cycling Proficiency Scheme (NCPS). Another scheme is the Right Track Cycling Awareness Programme – a training scheme developed by the Royal Society for the Prevention of Accidents (RoSPA). These courses are aimed at children between 9 and 12 years old and are usually arranged through schools. They teach children the basics in cycling skills for riding on the road and teach them to recognise the dangers of traffic. They also cover general bicycle maintenance, control skills, road manoeuvres and the Highway Code.

In some parts of the country, Road Safety Officers run a local training course. For details of courses in your area, contact the Road Safety Officer at your local authority. He or she will also be able to provide general information on cycle safety.

CYCLE HELMETS

For around 70 per cent of cyclists who are killed on British roads each year, head injury is a major cause of death. Yet more than three-quarters of all cyclists do not own a cycle helmet. While there can be no substitute for safe riding practice and good road sense, wearing a properly fitted cycle helmet could help prevent or reduce the severity of head injuries in the event of an accident.

Types of helmet

Cycle helmets work on the principle of absorbing shock from the impact of a bump or crash and distributing the force over a larger area. They cost around £12 to £30 and are available in three basic types. The difference is in the shell that surrounds the protective liner of expanded polystyrene or polypropylene.

Hard-shell helmets are generally heavier than other types, but protect the wearer's head from sharp objects and can withstand more everyday wear-and-tear. They provide the best all-round protection.

Thin-shell (micro-shell) helmets weigh less than hard-shell helmets, but don't give such good protection against sharp objects, although they can withstand normal wear-and-tear.

No-shell helmets normally have a removable Lycra mesh cover over the liner. They are the lightest helmet you can buy, but can't offer the same protection against sharp objects as the other types, and they scuff and mark easily.

Approved helmets

In addition to the British Standard, three international standards are widely accepted in the UK. When buying a cycle helmet always choose one that conforms to at least one of the following safety standards:

- BS 6863:1989 - the British Standard
- ANSI Z 90.4 - the official US standard
- SNELL B90 - a particularly high standard developed by an American non-profit organisation promoting helmet safety
- AS 2063.86 - the official Australian standard

Helmets which also have a BSI Kitemark, or AS or SNELL Foundation sticker are subjected to regular testing by those organisations, giving additional assurance that they are of a consistently high quality.

How to choose

The most important thing to remember when choosing a helmet, for yourself or your children, is to try before you buy. Fit and comfort are very important.

- Buy the smallest size of helmet that gives a snug fit. With straps adjusted, the helmet should not move backwards or forwards, or from side to side.
- Make sure it has an inner layer of crushable, expanded polystyrene or polypropylene.
- Check that the helmet or the adjustable straps don't cover your ears.
- Make sure the straps are secure when fastened. All straps should be

equally tight and free from slack and should not come undone easily, except when you press the quick-release buckle (if fitted).
- It is important that the helmet does not restrict your hearing or vision.
- Make sure there are adequate ventilation holes and internal channels to provide a cooling air flow, especially to the forehead.
- Style, though not one of the most critical issues, is still a factor, especially when buying for children. You don't want them taking their helmet off as soon as they're out of your sight!

Replacing a damaged helmet
You should buy a new helmet if you have an accident even if the old one doesn't look damaged.

All helmets should be replaced after a few years, even if they have been carefully used. This is particularly important for children.

BE SAFE, BE SEEN

As a cyclist it is essential that you are clearly visible to motorists and other road users day and night.

Cyclists are vulnerable road users particularly after dark. According to the most recent Department of Transport figures (1993), commuting cyclists and those riding at night are most at risk. Almost half of all cycling casualties reported each year occur between 5pm and 9am. In many accidents involving collisions with vehicles, drivers claim they didn't see cyclists in time, so make sure they can see you.

Cycle lights and reflectors
All new bikes must by law be equipped with at least one front and rear light and a rear reflector, all in good working order. These must be BS approved. Lights *must* be used when cycling at night between sunset and sunrise and during the day when visibility is seriously reduced. It's easier to remember that when street lights are on, and drivers are using their lights, you switch yours on too.

There are two main types of cycle lighting available. Each has its own advantages:

Battery-operated lights are the most widely available and most commonly used. They are cheap to buy (around £15–£25) and usually are easy to fit. If you ride regularly at night, however, you may find that the cost of replacement batteries mounts up. One solution to this is to invest in a set of rechargeable batteries and a charger. Bear in mind that lights which run on larger batteries are heavier but are more reliable if you ride at night for more than half an hour regularly.

Dynamo lights are the most economical, as they are relatively inexpensive to buy and cost practically nothing to run. But remember, they only produce light when the bike is moving and dim when you go slowly or stop at junctions and traffic lights. So either use a battery back-up unit, or walk your bike through difficult junctions where you normally have to slow down or stop.

Cycle light tips

Before buying cycle lights, make sure that they conform to BS 6102/3 or BS 3648 for rear lights. Choose lights which can be easily fixed on to your bike. Both front and rear lights should be securely mounted centrally or on the right-hand side of the bicycle so that they are clearly visible. Make sure they're not positioned too high or low – legally both front and rear lights should be mounted at least 35 cm/14 in and not more than 150 cm/59 in from the ground. Front lights should be angled slightly downwards.

Warning

The new battery LED (light-emitting diodes) cycle lights are bright and are cheap to run. They work by emitting a fast flash rather than a constant stream of light so that their batteries last up to four times longer than on normal lights. However, they currently don't meet the British Standard and are illegal if used without other lights.

- Front lights must be white and marked BS 6102/3. They should provide a good, bright, penetrating beam with sufficient light spread to illuminate the road in front of you and also to warn oncoming traffic or pedestrians.
- Rear lights must be red so that they don't dazzle other road users. They should conform to BS 3648 or BS 6102/3. Look for a rear light with a large lens to ensure good light spread.
- Choose cycle lights with either halogen or krypton bulbs. The gases inside the bulb provide a brighter beam compared with standard bulbs.
- Always carry a spare set of new or fully charged batteries, and spare bulbs with you. This is especially important on long rides, or if you use rechargeable batteries, which can fade quite suddenly when the charge is exhausted.
- Check that your lights are shining brightly. Replace batteries if the light is getting weak. Remove batteries if they're not in regular use. Regularly clean lights and reflectors.

Reflectors

There are many different reflectors you can fit to your bicycle. Reflectors are very good for helping drivers see you in the dark because they appear to 'light up' and reflect light back to the driver when headlights shine on them. They don't work when they are dirty, so keep them clean, and remember, lights must also be fitted.

- By law, a red rear reflector and white front reflector must be fitted on your bike at the point of sale – but they are not legally obligatory in use. They should be fitted centrally or on the right-hand side. The large wide-angle reflectors are best.
- Wheel or spoke reflectors are fitted to all new bicycles. They should preferably be white or amber, and if you have more than one, don't mix the colours. Reflective tyres can also be used. They show up well in car headlights when side-on.
- All bicycles made after 1 October 1985 are fitted with amber pedal reflectors. They can be fitted to most pedals if you don't already have

them. They show up very well in the dark, as they are low enough to pick up the beam from vehicle headlights, and they move up and down.

- Bike spacer flags or rods are horizontal rods with a flag or reflector attached. They are fitted to the rear of the bike to encourage drivers to leave more space when overtaking cyclists. If you use a bike spacer, make sure it is fixed securely.

- All reflectors must be marked BS 6102/2.

Reflective and fluorescent clothing

To make sure you can be seen by other road users, wear brightly coloured clothes. The best option is clothing that is both fluorescent (for day-time wear) and reflective (for night-time wear). If you don't have anything fluorescent or reflective, at least wear something bright or light coloured. Whatever you do, don't go out at night in dark clothes. Remember, cyclists who are seen are less likely to be hurt.

Fluorescent material is special bright material that shows up well in daylight but is not effective at night. It reacts with the ultraviolet rays in the sunlight, which makes it glare. Usually yellow or orange, fluorescent anoraks, waistcoats and jerseys are all available. But remember, fluorescent fabrics tend to fade over a period of time.

Reflective material is only effective at night when its special surface reflects the light from car headlights straight back to the driver, causing it to shine. The most noticeable garments are fluorescent jackets with reflective strips round the sleeves and body. Bibs, ankle bands, armbands, sashes and belts are quite effective too. You can also buy reflective strips to sew or stick on to your clothing or bike. Often cycling shoes or trainers have reflective patches on the heels.

Mini LED (light-emitting diode) lights designed to be attached to belts, cycle helmets or backpacks, and reflective bands incorporating flashing LEDs, are worth considering. These also act as reflectors when the lights are switched off.

CYCLE SAFETY TIPS

- Make sure your bike is the right size with the saddle and handlebars in the correct position.
- Check that your bike is roadworthy. Look after it, paying special attention to brakes and lights. Make sure your tyres are properly inflated and you can clearly see the tread – worn tyres won't grip the road well in the wet. Carry a pump, a puncture repair kit and a spare inner tube. Make sure you know how to repair a puncture.
- Be seen – wear bright clothing so that other road users can see you clearly. And remember to use cycle lights at night; it's the law.
- Be heard – fix a bell on your bike and use it to warn pedestrians against wandering across your path.
- Wear a cycle helmet.
- Children should go on a cycle training course and practise with an adult.
- When cycling on roads, be confident. Ride at least a metre (yard) from the kerb so you are clearly visible to other road users. Use cycle lanes if provided.
- Be alert. Concentrate, try to anticipate what's going to happen ahead and think safety – don't take unnecessary risks. Look where you're going, and watch out for pedestrians crossing between vehicles. Don't ride straight off the pavement on to the road. Never swerve to avoid an obstacle without making sure it is safe to do so.
- Signal clearly before you change direction – always know what's going on behind you. If you feel a junction is hazardous, get off and cross on foot.
- Play safe – two-thirds of young children are hurt by doing tricks or playing. Keep both hands on the handlebars: bikes aren't toys. And they should only be ridden by one person at a time!
- Be careful not to overload your bike. You're safer with your belongings in a saddlebag or panniers, with the weight equally balanced on either side. Make sure nothing is loose which can catch in the wheels or chain. Don't carry anything so you can keep your hands free to signal and control your bike.

ENCOURAGING SAFER CYCLING

Campaigning groups representing cyclists are demanding better education for all road users, and greater investment in schemes to reduce accidents and to encourage more cycling. You can get more information about local groups in your area from the Cycle Campaign Network.

USEFUL ADDRESSES

Animal Aunts
Wydwooch
45 Fairview Road
Headley Down
Hampshire GU35 8HQ
Tel: 01428 712611

Antiques Trade Gazette
17 Whitcomb Street
London WC2H 7PL
Tel: 0171 930 7195

The Art and Antiques Recording Service
Control Risks Group
83 Victoria Street
London SW1H 0HW
Tel: 0171 222 1552

Art Loss Register
13 Grosvenor Place
London SW1X 7HH
Tel: 0171 235 3393

Association of British Insurers
51 Gresham Street
London EC2V 7HQ
Send a stamped self-addressed envelope

Association of Cycle Traders
31a High Street
Tunbridge Wells
Kent TN1 1XN
Tel: 01892 526081

Automobile Association (AA)
'Women on Wheels Workshop'
Norfolk House
Priestley Road
Basingstoke
Hampshire RG24 9NY
AA information helpline
Tel: 0161 485 6000

Britannia Rescue
'Safe Driver Initiative'
St George's Square
Huddersfield
West Yorkshire HD1 1JF
Tel: 01484 514848

British Association of Toy Retailers
(BATR)
24 Baldwyn Gardens
London W3 6HL
Tel: 0181 993 2894

British Blind and Shutter Association
42 Heath Street
Tamworth
Staffordshire B79 7JH
Tel: 01827 52337

British Carpet Manufacturers'
Association
5 Portland Place
London W1N 3AA
Tel: 0171 580 7155

British Cycling Federation & British
  Mountain Bike Federation
National Cycling Centre
1 Stuart Street
Manchester M11 4DQ
Tel: 0161 223 2244

British Red Cross
9 Grosvenor Crescent
London SW1X 7EJ
Tel: 0171 235 5454

British Security Industry Association
Security House
Barbourne Road
Worcester WR1 1RS
Tel: 01905 21464

British Toy & Hobby Association
  (BTHA)
80 Camberwell Road
London SE5 0EG
Tel: 0171 701 7271

Child Accident Prevention Trust
4th Floor
Clerks Court
18–20 Farringdon Lane
London EC1R 3AU
Tel: 0171 608 3828

Childcheck
PO Box 1792
Christchurch
Dorset BH23 4YR
Send a stamped self-addressed envelope

Cope and Timmins Ltd
Angel Road Works
Edmonton
London N18 3AY
Send a stamped self-addressed envelope

The Cot Death Society
1 Browning Close
Thatcham
Newbury
Berks RG13 4AU
Tel: 01635 861771

Council for Registered Gas Installers
  (CORGI)
4 Elmwood
Chineham Business Park
Crockford Lane
Basingstoke
Hampshire RG24 8WG
Tel: 01256 707060

Crime Concern
Signal Point
Station Road
Swindon
Wiltshire SN1 1FE
Tel: 01793 514596

Cycle Campaign Network
54–57 Allison Street
Digbeth
Birmingham B5 5TH
Send a stamped self-addressed envelope

Cyclists' Touring Club
Cotterill House
69 Meadrow
Godalming
Surrey GU7 3HS
Tel: 01483 417217

Electrical Contractors' Association
34 Palace Court
Bayswater
London W2 4HY
Tel: 0171 229 1266

Fire Protection Association
140 Aldersgate Street
London EC1A 4HX
Tel: 0171 606 3757

The Foundation for the Study of Infant
    Deaths (FSID)
14 Halkin Street
London SW1X 7DP
Tel: 0171 235 0965
Cot Death Helpline –
Tel: 0171 235 1721 (24 hour)

Glass and Glazing Federation
44–48 Borough High Street
London SE1 1XB
Tel: 0171 403 7177

Help the Aged
St James's Walk
London EC1R 0BE
Tel: 0171 253 0253

The Home Office
Crack Crime
PO Box 999
Sudbury
Suffolk CO10 6FS
Send a stamped self-addressed envelope

Homesitters Ltd
Buckland Wharf
Buckland
Aylesbury
Bucks HP22 5LQ
Tel: 01296 630730

In-Car Safety Centre
Unit 5
The Auto Centre
Stacey Bushes
Milton Keynes MK12 6HS
Tel: 01908 220909

Kidscape
152 Buckingham Palace Road
London SW1W 9TR
Tel: 0171 730 3300

Laminated Glass Information Centre
299 Oxford Street
London W1R 1LA
Tel: 0171 499 1720

London Cycling Campaign
3 Stamford Street
London SE1 9NT
Tel: 0171 928 7220

Master Locksmiths Association
Unit 4/5
The Business Park
Woodford Halse
Daventry
Northamptonshire NN11 3PZ
Tel: 01327 262255

National Approval Council for Security
 Systems (NACOSS)
Queensgate House
14 Cookham Road
Maidenhead
Berkshire SL6 8AJ
Tel: 01628 37512

National Inspection Council for
 Electrical Installation Contracting
Vintage House
37 Albert Embankment
London SE1 7UJ
Tel: 0171 582 7746

National Toy Council
c/o 1 Chelsea Manor Gardens
London SW3 5PN
Send a stamped self-addressed envelope

Nationwide Property Register Ltd
Focus House
95–97 Beverley Road
Kingston-upon-Hull
North Humberside HU3 1XY
Tel: 01482 28120

New Scotland Yard
Community Affairs Branch
Broadway
London SW1H 0BG
Tel: 0171 230 3273

RAC
'Women's Workshops'
PR Department
RAC House
Brent Terrace
London NW2 1LT
Send a stamped self-addressed envelope

Re-Solv
30a High Street
Stone
Staffordshire ST15 8AW
Tel: 01785 817885

(Römer Vario)
Britax
1 Churchill Way West
Andover
Hampshire SP10 3UW
Tel: 01264 333343

Royal National Institute for Deaf People
105 Gower Street
London WC1E 6AH
Tel: 0171 387 8033

Royal Society for the Prevention of
 Accidents (RoSPA)
Cannon House
The Priory
Queensway
Birmingham B4 6BS
Tel: 0121 200 2461

SAS Security Products
Chestnut House
Chesley Hill
Wick
Nr. Bristol BS15 5NE
Tel: 0117 937 4737

Securicor TrakBak
Berkshire House
County Park
Shrivenham Road
Swindon
Wiltshire SN1 2NR
Tel: 01793 512848

Selectamark Security Systems Ltd
The Gatehouse
5 Locks Court
429 Crofton Road
Locksbottom
Kent BR6 8NL
Tel: 01689 860757

Simba Security Systems
Security House
Occupation Road
Walworth
London SE17 3BE
Tel: 0171 703 0485

(Slipsafe)
BTC
409 Victory Business Centre
Somers Road North
Portsmouth PO1 1PJ
Tel: 01705 861622

Smart Driving
Freepost (BS 8082)
4 Boyces Avenue
Clifton Village
Bristol BS8 4AA
Tel: 0117 970 6667

Sold Secure Office
Block 36
Northumbria Police HQ
Ponteland
Newcastle-upon-Tyne NE20 0BL
Tel: 01661 868446

St John Ambulance
1 Grosvenor Crescent
London SW1X 7EF
Tel: 0171 235 5231

The Suzy Lamplugh Trust
14 East Sheen Avenue
London SW14 8AS
Send a stamped self-addressed envelope

Trace
Mill Court
Furrlongs
New Port
Isle of Wight PO30 2AA
Tel: 01983 826000

Universal Aunts
PO Box 304
London SW4 0NN
Tel: 0171 738 8937

Victim Support
Cranmer House
39 Brixton Road
London
SW96DZ
Tel: 0171 735 9166

Waso Ltd
Alliance Close
Alliance Business Park
Nuneaton
Warwickshire CV11 6SD
Tel: 01203 352222

INDEX